101
Pistol Run Plays

James Vint

©2012 Coaches Choice. All rights reserved. Printed in the United States.

No part of this book may be reproduced, stored in a retrieval system, or transmitted, in any form or by any means, electronic, mechanical, photocopying, recording, or otherwise, without the prior permission of Coaches Choice. Throughout this book, the masculine shall be deemed to include the feminine and vice versa.

ISBN: 978-1-60679-224-7
Library of Congress Control Number: 2012938815
Cover design: Studio J Art & Design
Book layout: Studio J Art & Design
Front cover photo: ©Bob Falcetti/Icon SMI/ZUMA Press

Coaches Choice
P.O. Box 1828
Monterey, CA 93942
www.coacheschoice.com

Dedication

This book is dedicated to the great men who have impacted me throughout my life: James Vint Sr., Thomas F. Vint, Jack Combs, Dr. Charles Daniel, and Cicero Daniel.

Acknowledgments

This book would not be possible without many people who have been role models and mentors who have provided me with tremendous encouragement and support. First and foremost, I want to thank God, for making the ultimate sacrifice so we could have eternal salvation. Without Him, nothing would be possible.

My mother and father, Sandra and James Sr., provided me with a tremendous upbringing, and I cannot ever thank them enough. My wife, Mary Blake, was wonderful as she supported me through this entire process that required long nights and sore fingers. Jim Peterson helped guide me through the process and helped set this all into motion. Kristi Huelsing and Angie Perry were patient and supportive from start to finish. My coaching mentors, David Diaz and Jerry Campbell, encouraged me throughout the writing of this book.

I have been blessed to work with great coaches who are an inspiration to those around them. Kent Jackson, Mike Meeks, Blake Sandford, and Mark Ball bring out the best in kids and other coaches. My high school football coach, Craig Parkinson, has been a mentor to me throughout my coaching career.

Contents

Dedication 3

Acknowledgments 4

Preface 6

Chapter 1: Formations and Motions 7

Chapter 2: Inside Zone Play 12

Chapter 3: Inside Seal Concept 20

Chapter 4: Inside Lead Concept 35

Chapter 5: Power Concept 48

Chapter 6: Sweep Concept 64

Chapter 7: Isolation Concept 78

Chapter 8: Trap Concept 94

Chapter 9: Counter Concept 106

Chapter 10: Belly Concept 115

Chapter 11: Reverses and Special Plays 123

About the Author 133

Preface

I have had the opportunity to coach football during three different decades. Our profession is unique in that so many are willing to share their knowledge and experience. Because of the hard work of so many coaches, I have had the good fortune of being able to learn some concepts that we have had some success with at both the high school and college levels. It is a pleasure to be able to share these concepts with others.

My hope with this book is that each of you can take some of what is written on the following pages and apply it to your program. This volume is by no means an exhaustive book of plays that can be run in the pistol. It is, however, a collection of 101 of our most successful pistol run plays. If this book helps you put more points on the scoreboard, it will be considered a success.

1

Formations and Motions

The pistol offense gives you an opportunity to run multiple formations with diverse personnel groups. By using multiple formations, the offense can keep the defense off-balance. Your ultimate goal is to gain leverage on the defense at the point of attack. By using a variety of formations, you can force the defense to have to make adjustments, rather than simply lining up in their base front.

One of the biggest dilemmas facing coaches is how to keep the verbiage simple. Play calls can get very wordy. Because of this, the formations will be kept short using a word and a number. The word identifies the strength and type of formation. The number tells the fullback where he will align. Your fullback will be your adjuster in the pistol offense.

If the word in the formation begins with an R, the strength of the formation will be to the right. If the word in the formation begins with L, the strength will go to the left. The number in the formation call tells the fullback where he will align. The numbers correspond somewhat with traditional hole numbering. The following shows the different alignments for the fullback based on the number called. Because the tight end is to the right, the formation would be named with an R word.

In the pistol, the offensive line will use two-foot splits. However, you can adjust these splits as needed based on the concepts you are running. The quarterback will align at 4.5 yards from the center. Doing so gives the quarterback depth in the pass game, while allowing him to execute the entire run game effectively. The tailback will align directly behind the quarterback at eight yards. His depth can be adjusted as needed. When you install any offensive system, it is important to remember these are just guidelines. There are teaching alignments, and then there are ability alignments. Ability alignments are adjustments you will make based on the ability of your players. Be flexible so you can take advantage of the strengths of your personnel.

The base formation set with a tight end in the game is Rip/Liz. Rip puts the tight end to the right with his hand down. Liz puts the tight end to the left. By adding a number based on the example in Figure 1-1, the fullback will be told where to line up. Rip 2 puts the tight end to the right and the fullback lined up behind the right tackle. Rip 4 would put the fullback aligned one yard outside the tight end and one yard off the line of scrimmage. Liz would move the tight end to the left side of the formation. In Figure 1-2, the call is Rip 2. Rip puts the tight end to the right with his hand down. The number 2 tells the fullback to align at the depth of the quarterback, directly behind the right offensive tackle.

In addition to Rip and Liz, other words can be used to change the position of the Y. Ron and Lou align the Y as a twin receiver, off the line of scrimmage. Ray and Lee tell the Y to line up as a tight end, and the X and Z both to align opposite the tight end. This is the typical twins closed look. R and L align the Y as a slot. Finally, Rex and Lex tell the offense you are aligning in a bunch set. Figure 1-3 shows Lou 6, which is a typical 2x2 formation call for the offense.

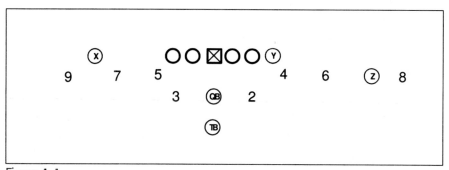
Figure 1-1

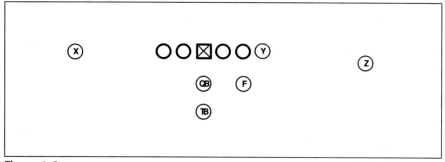
Figure 1-2

If the offense wanted to line up in a trips formation, they would put the fullback and the Y to the same side. Using Rip/Liz or Ron/Lou, the offense can align in a trips formation to either side. Rip 6 puts the fullback as a twin receiver to the side of the tight end, as displayed in Figure 1-4.

As you can see, aligning in a variety of formations is very simple. This system allows the offense to communicate hundreds of formation concepts with very simple verbiage. You can align in any formation imaginable using this system of R and L words combined with numbers. You can also tag special formations. Wing tells the Z to align one yard outside the tight end, one yard off the line of scrimmage. Figure 1-5 shows Liz 3 wing.

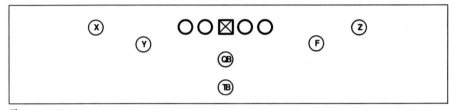

Figure 1-3

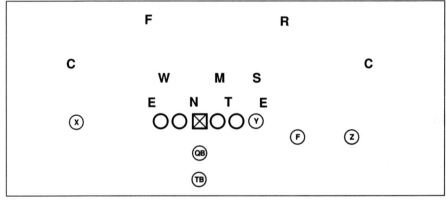

Figure 1-4

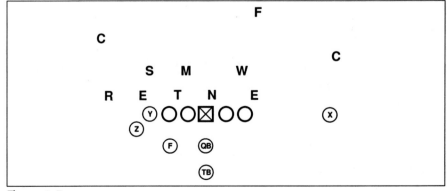

Figure 1-5

Once you have set your formations, you will need to have a simple way to use motion. You need to incorporate motion into your offense for several reasons:
- Force the defense to declare their coverage.
- Gain leverage on a defender.
- Force the defense to flip personnel.
- Make the defense change their strength.
- Create a mismatch.
- Flood one side of the field.
- Remove a defender from the point of attack.
- Bring an additional blocker to the point of attack.

Communicating motion can be very simple for you and your coaches. The system you will see depicted is very simple for communicating motion with players. This system is phonetic, which often is much easier for players to remember. Despite being simple, it has a built-in way to communicate movement for nearly every skill player.

Y Motions

- *Trade*: Flips the Y from one side to the other
- *Yip:* Y into the formation
- *Yap:* Y across the formation
- *Yop:* Y to the outside

Z Motions

- *Zip:* Z into the formation
- *Zap:* Z across the formation
- *Zop:* Z to the outside

Fullback Motions

- *Fip:* Fullback into the formation
- *Fap:* Fullback across the formation
- *Fop:* Fullback to the outside
- *Fox:* Fullback outside the X
- *Foz:* Fullback outside the Z

T Motions

- *Tip:* Tailback into the formation
- *Tap:* Tailback across the formation
- *Top:* Tailback to the outside
- *Tox:* Tailback outside the X
- *Toz:* Tailback outside the Z

As you can see, the motion terminology is very consistent from one position to the next. This makes it very easy for skill players to be able to play multiple positions. Ultimately, you want to keep things simple, allowing your athletes to play fast. In Figure 1-6, you will see zap motion, which tells the Z to go across the formation. The call in the huddle would be Rip 2 zap.

With this simple phonetic system, you can put any of your skill players in motion from anywhere on the field. This system allows your players to align in multiple positions and not have to learn a new motion call for each position. If you want to motion the fullback to the outside, you would tag the motion as fop, which is depicted in Figure 1-7.

Making your formation and motion rules simple allows you to be able to be multiple on offense. This allows you to gain leverage on the defense at the point of attack. You can use virtually any word you want to communicate with your players about where to line up. By keeping your formation and motion system simple, you will be more multiple on offense. You force defenses to have more to prepare for each week. The more a defense has to prepare for, the less time they have to spend on each aspect of your offense.

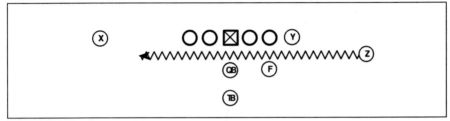

Figure 1-6

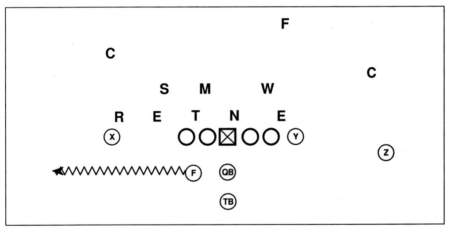

Figure 1-7

2

Inside Zone Play

The inside zone play allows you to attack multiple gaps with a single blocking scheme. Perhaps the most important aspect of the inside zone is the simplicity for the offensive line. If your offensive line can count to three, they can identify the area they will block and the player they will key on defense.

The concept of the inside zone is that each offensive lineman will be responsible for blocking an area rather than a man. Adding a count system allows each offensive lineman to be on the same page. They will have a better understanding of which defenders they will key as they track through their area.

Inside Zone Blocking Rules and Mechanics

The count system is as easy as 0-1-2-3. The first key is the center identifying who the zero is. The zero is defined as the first defender on or over the center to the playside. If no player is on or over the center, the zero will be the first defender to the playside. Once the center comes to the line of scrimmage, he draws an imaginary line down the center of the defense. Figure 2-1 illustrates the imaginary line the center draws through the center of the defense.

Once the center draws a line down the middle of the defense, he identifies and communicates who the zero is. Once he identifies who the zero is, the offensive linemen then count to 3 on each side of the zero. The zero is the first player on or over the center to the playside. The zero can be a defensive lineman or a linebacker. Figure 2-2 illustrates the count system.

The offensive line rules for the inside zone are very simple. They are outlined as follows:
- The center has playside A gap to zero.
- The playside guard has playside B gap to number 1.
- The playside tackle has playside C gap to number 2.
- The tight end has playside D gap to number 3.
- The backside guard has backside A gap to number 1 backside.
- The backside tackle has backside B gap to number 2 backside.
- The fullback has backside number 3, unless he is tagged to block another player.

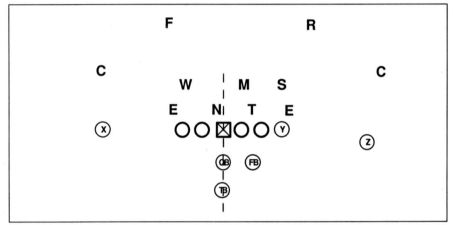
Figure 2-1

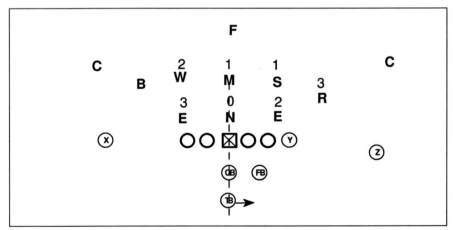
Figure 2-2

Once the offensive line understands their rules and the count system, they can play fast and hard. Because the play is simple, the offensive line can easily make in-game adjustments. The inside zone play can ensure your offensive line always has a hat on every run defender.

The count system for the inside zone means you can easily account for a variety of defensive fronts. Figure 2-3 illustrates the count versus the college 4-3 solid defense.

Figure 2-4 illustrates the count system for the under defense. In addition to blocking even fronts, this count system can be used to block odd fronts as well. Figure 2-5 illustrates an example of the 5-2 or 3-4 Eagle weak defense.

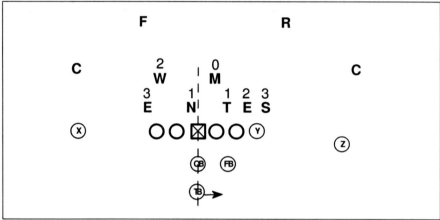

Figure 2-3

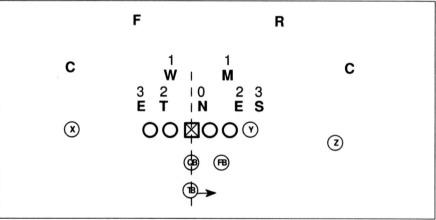

Figure 2-4

This simple count system also works very well to account for each defender in the 3-3 stack. When the defense stacks a linebacker over a down player, the linebacker will be assigned the lower number. Against the 3-3 stack, the nose will be the zero. The Mike will actually be the backside number 1. Figure 2-6 shows how the count system would work versus a 3-3 stack.

Once you have identified the zero and counted to three on the frontside and backside, the offensive line is ready to actually make their blocks. The aiming point for the offensive line is the playside jersey number of the defensive player. The offensive lineman will adjust his footwork to make sure he can reach his landmark.

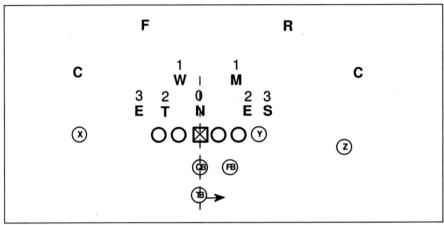

Figure 2-5

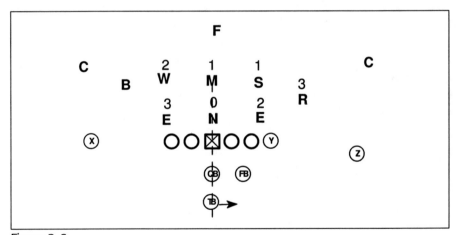

Figure 2-6

The offensive line must be able to reach and overtake a slanting defensive lineman into their gap responsibility. The wider the threat to their gap, the deeper their first step will be. Conversely, the tighter the threat to their gap, the flatter their first step will be.

The first step the offensive linemen will take is called a base step. Their base step is vital to get them to their landmark. Their second step is called the power step. The power step is just as it sounds. It is designed to put the offensive linemen in a position to deliver a powerful blow to the playside jersey number of the defender.

If you are running zone to the right, your offensive lineman will take a six-inch step with his right foot. He will then take his second step with his left foot, aiming for the crotch of the defender. His third step will be with his right foot again, working to the playside jersey number of the defender.

In addition to understanding zone footwork, your offensive linemen must be able to work in combination with one another. The most popular way to work zone combinations is to have your covered player working with an uncovered offensive lineman. Zone combination blocking puts two offensive linemen working in tandem tracking a down defender to linebacker. While this takes practice and repetition, it ensures you will be able to account for any defensive front you may face.

When you work a zone combination block, your two linemen working in tandem must communicate with each other before the ball is snapped. They must each echo the call to make sure they know they are working together. If your guard and tackle are working together, they will most likely be working to a 4 or 5 technique. A 4 technique is identified as being head-up on the tackle, and a 5 technique is playing an outside shade on the tackle. The alignment of the down defender will predicate the depth of the first step of both of your offensive linemen. If the down defender slants to the B gap, the guard will block him, and the tackle will climb to linebacker. If the down defender stays in the C gap, the tackle will block him. Your guard will then climb to linebacker. Figure 2-7 illustrates the combination block with an uncovered lineman working with a covered lineman.

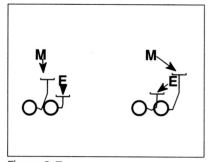

Figure 2-7

Figures 2-8 through 2-12 show which linemen will be working together against several different fronts. It is vital your linemen understand the importance of communicating before the snap on each and every play. Figure 2-8 illustrates the offensive linemen who will be working together against an over front. Figure 2-9 shows which offensive linemen will work together versus an overshift 4-3 defense.

Figure 2-10 shows the zone combination blocks versus an under front. The inside zone is also a very good play versus odd front defenses. Figure 2-11 illustrates zone combination blocks against a 3-4 defense. In Figure 2-12, inside zone combination blocks are illustrated against a 3-3 stack. The inside zone gives the offense the ability to account for each defender in a stacked defensive concept.

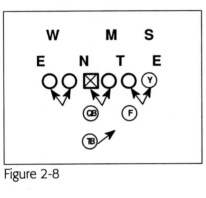

Figure 2-8

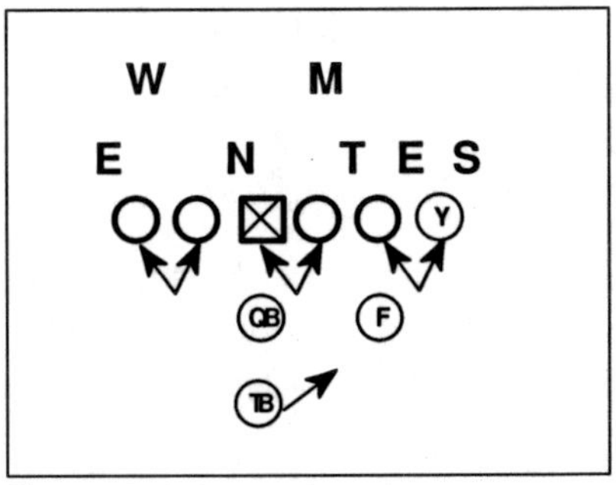

Figure 2-9

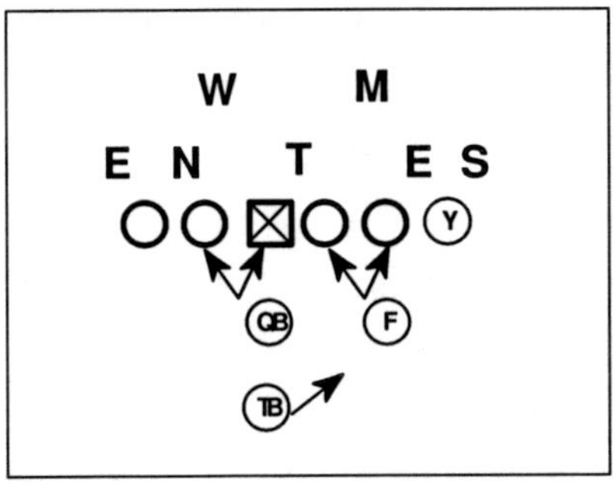

Figure 2-10

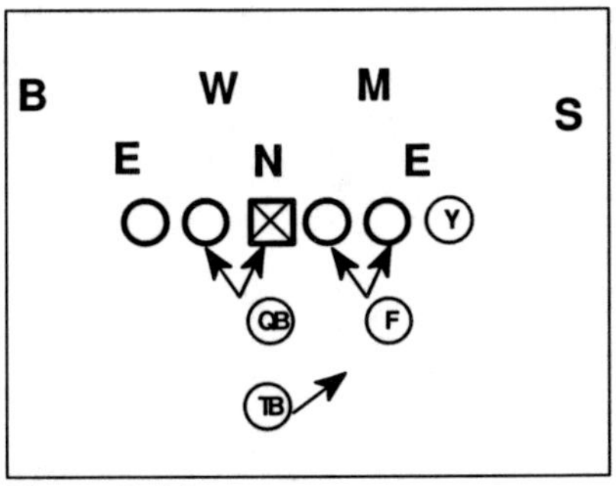

Figure 2-11

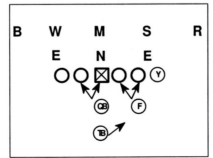

Figure 2-12

While your offensive line is vital to the overall success of the inside zone play, it is the blocking of the perimeter players that will result in game-breaking big plays. The blocking for the receivers is relatively simple. The playside wide receiver is responsible for the force player. His release will work inside at a 45-degree angle with his vision working to find the first secondary player responsible for forcing the run. The receiver will look to get inside number leverage on the defensive back, settle and punch, then run his feet. He must not allow the defensive back to make the play. It is vital to prepare your receivers so they are aware of defensive tendencies. This preparation will help them anticipate who they will block.

The backside receiver runs what is called a touchdown path. He will release immediately, working across the field at about a 45-degree angle. The backside receiver is going to run until a defender crosses his path. He must be careful to block the front of the defender and not clip. While you don't want your receivers to watch the play, you must coach them to be aware of the football at all times. Figure 2-13 illustrates the inside zone play to the right with perimeter blocking.

Now that you have a better understanding of the blocking rules, it is time to consider the running back and quarterback. For your traditional downhill zone play, the quarterback will open up to 4 o'clock and roll the ball back. Each quarterback has a clock when he takes a snap: 12 noon is straight ahead, and 6 o'clock is directly behind the quarterback. Once the quarterback steps to 4 o'clock, he will roll the ball back. You want him to work on a 45-degree angle to the running back and reach the ball into the running back's navel. The quarterback will then fake a boot opposite the play with his hands on his back hip, as if he is hiding the football.

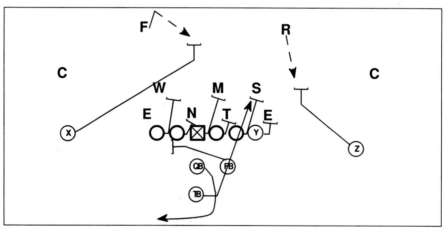

Figure 2-13

The running back will take a zone step at a 45-degree angle. This step is a flat step to the playside with his playside foot. Coach your running back to take a zone step and roll it over. You want him to work on a 45-degree angle to the mesh point with the quarterback. When the running back takes his zone step, he must be patient to give the quarterback time to secure the snap. The running back must have his eyes up throughout the entire play, watching the blocking of the offensive line.

Once the running back has the handoff, he attacks the outside hip of the offensive tackle. He is reading the first combination block to the playside. To keep it simple, you simply tell him to press the line and run to daylight. As your running back gets more experienced, you can give him the option of cutting the ball back. Coach your running back to be patient to the hole and explode through. One key coaching point is to make sure your running back's shoulders are parallel to the shoulders of your offensive linemen. If your offensive linemen are not blocking second-level players, it is most likely because your running back's shoulders are on a different plane than the offensive linemen.

The inside zone play is simple in concept, but complex for the defense to defend. The blocking rules are literally as easy as 0-1-2-3. Once your players understand their base rules and master the footwork, you are on your way to having a solid football play. The fun part comes as you begin to run different variations of the inside zone.

3

Inside Seal Concept

The base inside zone concept is the seal concept. This base zone play is blocked with your base zone rules. Seal tells your fullback he will block the backside C gap. The key point for the fullback is making sure he secures the C gap and does not let anyone inside of him. Your fullback will work through the inside shoulder of the C gap player. In game planning, you must determine who the C gap player will be. Most often, it will be the defensive end.

The seal concept can be run from a variety of formations. You can also incorporate any of your motion calls as well. Regardless of formation or pre-snap movement, the base rules of the play stay the same. Running inside seal from a variety of formations will make a very simple concept look more complex to the defense.

Play #1: Rip 2 Inside Seal Right

Description: This is the base inside zone play from the pistol. The formation is Rip 2, with Rip telling the tight end he is aligned on the line of scrimmage on the right side, and the 2 tells the fullback he will align in the 2 position. The 2 position is aligned at the depth of the quarterback stacked on the right offensive tackle. The seal tag tells your fullback he will be blocking the backside C gap. As you will see in Figure 3-1, the offensive line follows their inside zone rules, while the fullback seals the backside C gap.

Coaching Points:

- The offensive linemen must get to the playside jersey number of the down defender.
- You want your offensive line to keep their shoulders as square as possible.
- The fullback must dig out the C gap player. He cannot give up the inside.

Versus the 3-3 stack, the center will punch the nose to allow the backside guard to overtake the block. If the nose slants strong, the center will block him, and the backside guard will climb to the Mike linebacker. Figure 3-2 shows the inside seal play versus a 3-3 stack.

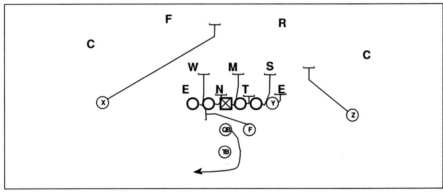

Figure 3-1

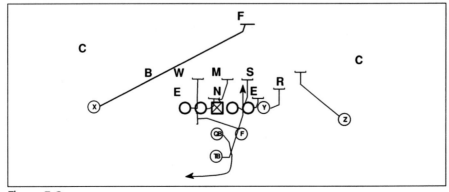

Figure 3-2

Play #2: Rip 4 Inside Seal Right

Description: Rip 4 puts the fullback aligned as a wing. You can use your fullback, or you can bring another tight end into the game. From the 4 position, the fullback can still seal the backside C gap. He must be quick off the snap of the ball. As you can see in Figure 3-3, the back must hug the heels of the offensive line. This creates a cross-key issue for the inside linebackers on defense.

Coaching Points:

- The back must be patient as he presses the line of scrimmage.
- The playside receiver must be quick to block the force player.
- The fullback must dig out the C gap player. He cannot give up the inside.

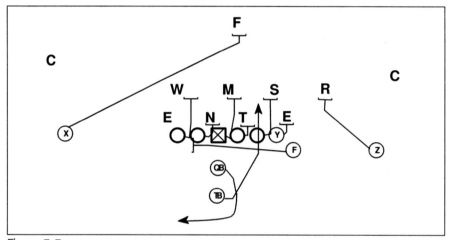

Figure 3-3

Play #3: Liz 2 Zap Seal Left

Description: Liz puts the tight end to the right side of the line, while the 2 puts the fullback to the right side. This would put the back to the weakside. Zap tells the Z-receiver he is going to motion across the formation. The mechanics of the play do not change. Motioning the Z-receiver would be used if the defense ran a defender with the motion, or if they rotated their secondary to motion.

Coaching Points:

- The Z must run full speed in motion.
- The quarterback should snap the ball when the Z-receiver gets halfway between the right tackle and the X.
- If the defense rotates with motion, the tailback may hit the edge for big yards.

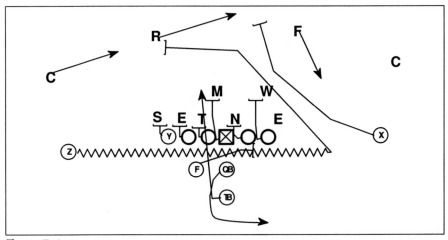

Figure 3-4

Play #4: Rip 8 Fip Inside Seal Right

Description: Rip 8 puts the fullback outside the X receiver. Fip motions the fullback into the formation. The quarterback will snap the ball when the fullback gets one yard outside the tight end. Essentially, you are motioning the fullback from the 8 position to the 4 position. This is an outstanding motion concept to use in the pass game, and using this motion concept in the run game will keep the defense off-balance.

Coaching Points:

- The Z will tighten his alignment when the fullback aligns outside him.
- The quarterback should snap the ball when the fullback is at the 4 position.
- The motion should be run at 70 percent of full speed.

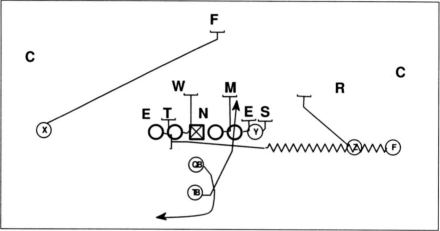

Figure 3-5

Play #5: Liz 9 Wing Inside Z Seal Left

Description: In addition to having the fullback seal the backside C gap, you can tag your Z to seal the backside C gap. Liz 9 wing is a three-man surface to the tight end with the fullback being split out wide and the Z being the wing. You can also put the fullback into motion across the formation to force the defense to adjust.

Coaching Points:

- The Z will align in a wing and seal the backside C gap, and he must have drill time.
- The must be drilled to block the force player.

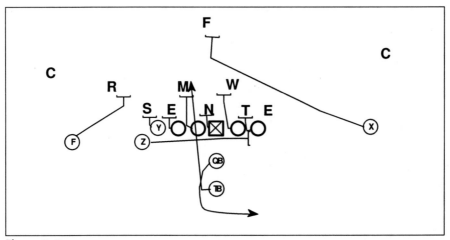

Figure 3-6

Play #6: L 3 Inside Seal Left

Description: L puts the Y flexed in a slot to the left side. The Y being flexed allows him to block the frontside or the backside. Flexing the Y also can help him release in your pass game. Nothing changes as far as the blocking rules for the offensive line.

Coaching Points:

- The Y still has playside C gap when he is flexed.
- The fullback will secure the backside C gap working inside out.
- Versus an under front, the tailback is reading off the first frontside combo.

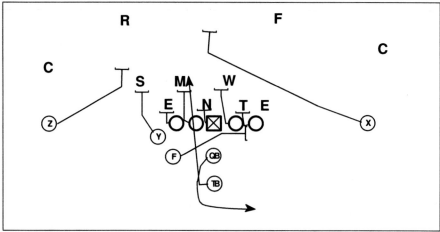

Figure 3-7

Play #7: Lou 2 Fap Inside Seal Left

Description: Lou puts the tight end in a twin position to the left side. The corresponding formation to the right side is Ron. The 2 aligns the fullback stacked over the right tackle at 4.5 yards. The fullback will go in motion to the left. He will shuffle and reset, or you can have the quarterback snap the ball as the fullback reaches the 3 position.

Coaching Points:

- The defense will most likely adjust to leverage your Y.
- If the defense doesn't adjust to your Y, use the bubble to attack the void.
- Your offensive line blocking rules do not change.

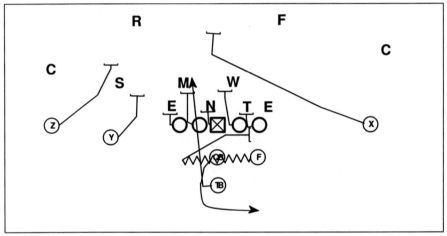

Figure 3-8

Play #8: Ron 3 Re-Fap Inside Seal Right

Description: Another variation of the inside seal is to motion the fullback across the other side wide, and bring him back to the 2 position. This is tagged as re-fap. This forces the defense to make a coverage check when the fullback widens, then check again when he works back inside the box. The blocking rules for the offensive line do not change.

Coaching Points:

- Your fullback must move quickly in motion to put pressure on the defense.
- Have one coach assigned to watch the defensive adjustment to motion.
- The mechanics of the play do not change.

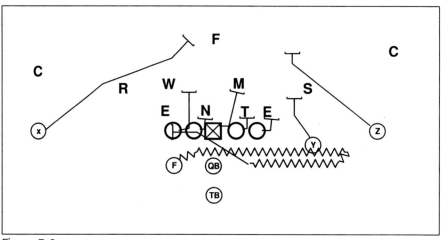

Figure 3-9

Play #9: Ron Bone Inside Seal Left Halfback Wheel

Description: The wishbone formation can be used from the pistol as well to give you a three-back look. This look forces the defense to put more players in the box. Ron bone gives you no tight end and leaves you two split receivers. You can either move your Y into the backfield, or bring another back into the game. The inside zone play is very good to run from the inverted bone. Because you are balanced, you can have the quarterback check the play either direction, based on the defense. There are a variety of options for your backs who are not getting the football. In Figure 3-10, the frontside back will seal the backside edge, while the backside back will run a wheel route. This action will hold the backside defensive player who is assigned the backside back.

Coaching Points:

- Your quarterback can check the play either way.
- Either offset back can be your seal player.
- The mechanics of the play are the same.

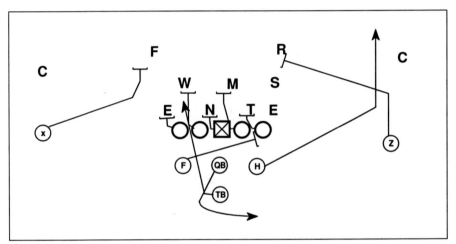

Figure 3-10

Play #10: Rip Bone X Over Inside Seal Left Halfback Wheel

Description: Rip or Liz bone leaves a tight end in the game. With X over, you will have your Y align as the weakside tackle, with both of your tackles aligned to the right side. The X must align on the line of scrimmage. You can either leave your Z in the game as the third back, or you can bring another running back into the game. It is good to have multiple personal groupings when you get into the bone so the defense cannot make calls based solely on personnel packages. The concept of the play is the exact same, keeping things very simple for your offensive line.

Coaching Points:

- The X must align on the line of scrimmage.
- Your tackles will go opposite the Rip/Liz call.
- The mechanics for the quarterback and tailback are the exact same.

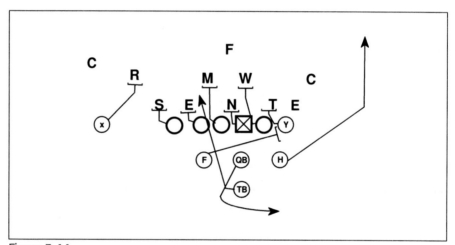

Figure 3-11

Play #11: Ron 2 Yip Inside Y Seal Left

Description: The inside zone play can also be run with the fullback. If the fullback is the ballcarrier, someone else will need to be the seal player. In Figure 3-12, the Y will motion into the formation and seal the backside C gap. When the fullback is running the zone, the quarterback will execute zone read footwork to mesh with the back. He will take a flat step to the back, then a short step with his back foot. His feet must not cross into the path of the back. He must reach the ball deep and ride the back through on the mesh. There is no read on this as it is a designed give. The quarterback and tailback will execute the pitch phase after the give to hold the backside.

Coaching Points:

- The fullback must work in front of the quarterback to take the handoff.
- The quarterback will ride the back.
- The offensive line uses inside zone blocking rules.

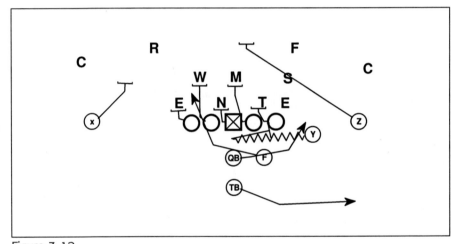

Figure 3-12

Play #12: Lou 2 Yip Inside Y Seal Right

Description: The inside zone can also be run with the fullback to the same side as he is set. Instead of working across the quarterback, he will take the handoff and work back to the side he was aligned. His read is the same, as he reads the first playside combination. This adds versatility to your run game, and keeps the defense off-balance. They never know who is getting the ball, or to which side you are running the zone play.

Coaching Points:

- The fullback will read the first frontside combination.
- The quarterback and tailback carry out a pitch phase fake after the give.
- The offensive line uses inside zone blocking rules.

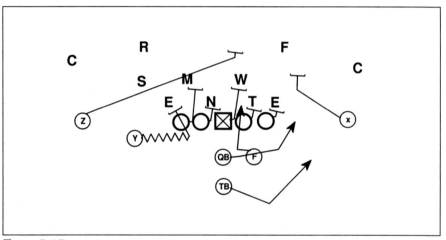

Figure 3-13

Play #13: Lou 2 Quarterback Inside Fullback Seal Right

Description: Working off the action with the fullback, the offense can have the quarterback keep the football and run the inside zone. The fullback will take the fake from the quarterback and seal the edge player. The quarterback will ride the fullback to hold the defense, before pulling the ball and working downhill. The offense will block the inside zone play to the direction the quarterback will run.

Coaching Points:

- The fullback will seal the backside C gap after taking the fake.
- The tailback will sprint to gain width to hold the edge defenders.
- The offensive line uses inside zone blocking rules.

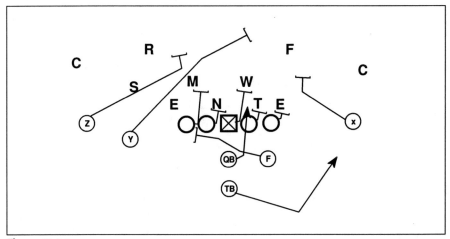

Figure 3-14

Play #14: Lou 2 Taz Inside Fullback Seal Right

Description: Taz is an alert you can use that says the quarterback will mesh with both backs. The quarterback will mesh with the fullback crossing in front of him, then he will pivot and mesh with the tailback crossing in front of him from the opposite side. The tailback must be patient to ensure the fullback has cleared the mesh point and the quarterback has time to pivot. After the quarterback gives the football to the tailback, he will sprint outside to hold the defense.

Coaching Points:

- The fullback will seal the backside C gap after taking the fake.
- The tailback will work downhill into the frontside bubble.
- The offensive line uses inside zone blocking rules.

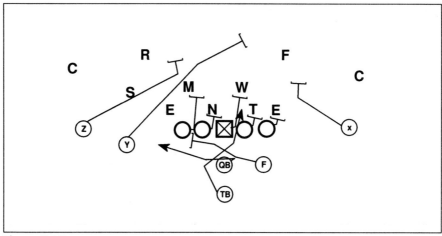

Figure 3-15

4

Inside Lead Concept

The two-back inside zone concept is the inside zone lead play. Instead of having your fullback block the backside C gap as he does in inside seal, the fullback will now block a frontside defender when you tag lead. The blocking rules for the offensive line do not change. However, they will make a small adjustment, depending on who the fullback will block.

The lead concept can be run from a variety of formations. You can also incorporate any of your motion calls as well. Regardless of formation or pre-snap movement, the base rules of the play do not change. Running the inside lead from a variety of formations will make a very simple concept look more complex to the defense.

Bob, Bomb, and Boss

When you install the inside lead, you have to communicate with the fullback who he will block. The defensive player the fullback is blocking must also be communicated with the offensive line to make sure everyone blocks the proper defender. You can have the fullback block a certain player by matchup or based on leverage. The most important aspect is that everyone gets blocked at the point of attack.

Bob: Bob stands for back on backside backer, which means the back will block the backside inside linebacker. This tells the player who normally blocks the backside backer that he can help the lineman next to him. In Figure 4-1, the bob block is illustrated versus an under front defense. The backside guard would normally have the backside inside backer, but with the bomb call, he will now alert the tackle that they will double-team the 3 technique.

Bomb: Bomb tells the fullback he will block the Mike or playside backer. With the bomb call, you are saying you want to block the linebacker at the point of attack on the frontside. Figure 4-2 shows the inside zone play with a bomb call versus an under front. The frontside guard would normally be responsible for the Mike backer, but with a bomb call, he now can double-team the 1 technique with the center.

Boss: Boss means back on strong safety. The boss call allows you to put the fullback on the alley player or edge player. The boss call is popular on both the inside and outside zone. Figure 4-3 illustrates the boss call. With a boss call, the playside receiver will vertical stalk the man over him. The fullback will arc to the Rover or strong safety.

Using bob, bomb, and boss allows you to change the leverage of your offensive line, while forcing the defense to defend the same play in a variety of looks. The concept of bob, bomb, and boss helps to clear the picture for accounting for extra defenders to the playside.

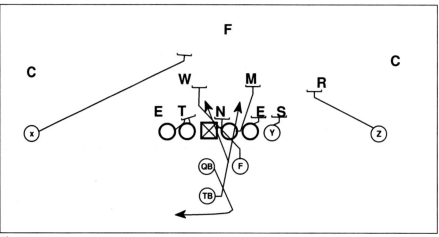

Figure 4-1

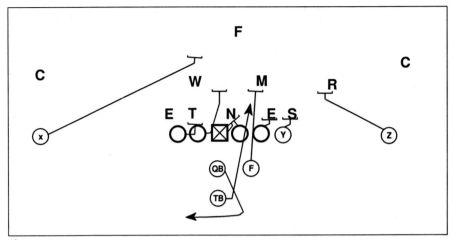

Figure 4-2

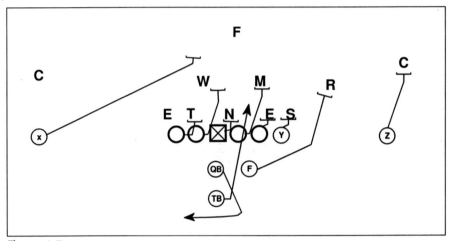

Figure 4-3

Play #15: Rip 2 Inside Lead Right (Bob)

Description: By tagging lead, you are telling the fullback he will block to the playside. This gives you a chance to get another offensive player at the point of attack. Figure 4-4 illustrates the inside lead play with a bob call versus an overshift 4-3 defense. The bob call versus an overshift 4-3 turns the inside zone into a downhill run play with a two-way go for the back. If the backside 1 technique plays hard to the frontside, the back will take it through the back door. If the 1 technique plays soft, the back will hit the frontside A gap downhill.

Coaching Points:

- The offensive linemen use their inside zone footwork and rules.
- The fullback will bend backside and work up to the backside backer.
- The tailback will read the block on the backside nose.

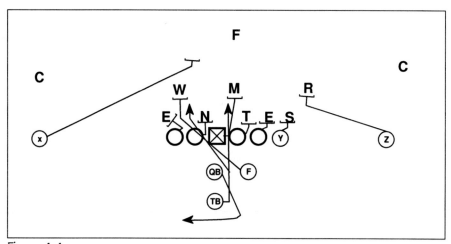

Figure 4-4

Play #16: Rip 4 Inside Lead Right (Boss)

Description: Rip 4 puts the fullback aligned as a wing. You can use your fullback, or you can bring another tight end into the game. From the 4 position, the fullback can block the edge or he can seal the playside linebacker. This gives you the opportunity to have another blocker at the point of attack. Figure 4-5 shows the fullback blocking the boss concept from a wing position versus an under front 4-3.

Coaching Points:

- The offensive line uses inside zone blocking rules and footwork.
- On a boss call, the playside receiver will vertical stalk block, blocking the man over him.
- The quarterback will boot fake after giving the football.

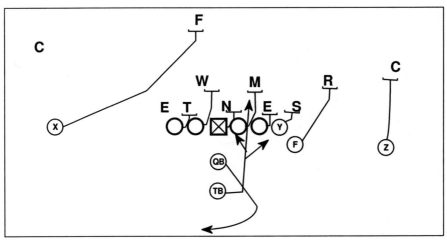

Figure 4-5

Play #17: Liz 5 Inside Lead Left (Bomb)

Description: Liz 5 puts the tight end to the left and the fullback in a wing position. With a bomb call, the fullback will fold inside and up to the Mike or playside backer. This allows the center and guard to combo the nose. The playside tackle now has a man block on the 5 technique. The tight end will have a man block on the Sam backer. The backside guard will climb to the backside linebacker. Figure 4-6 illustrates the bomb call from a wing position.

Coaching Points:

- The fullback must find the bubble to the playside.
- The offensive line will no longer have to track the Mike backer.
- This forces the playside inside backer to slow his flow.

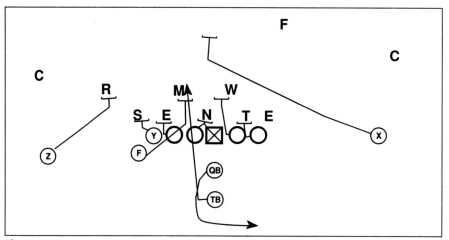

Figure 4-6

Play #18: Rip 8 Fip Inside Lead Right (Bomb)

Description: Rip 8 puts the fullback outside the X-receiver. Fip motions the fullback into the formation. The quarterback will snap the ball when the fullback gets to the tight end. The fullback will be two yards behind the line of scrimmage when the ball is snapped. The fullback will block the frontside inside backer. Aligning the fullback outside the box forces the defense to align to a variety of formations, then adjust once you motion. Figure 4-7 shows this concept versus an overshift 4-3.

Coaching Points:

- The Z will tighten his alignment when the fullback aligns outside him.
- The quarterback should snap the ball when the fullback gets to the tight end.
- The motion should be run at 70 percent of full speed.

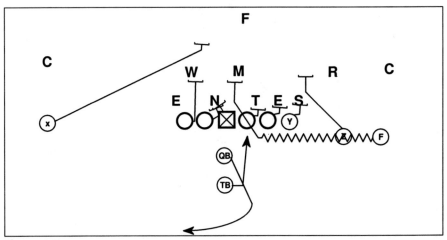

Figure 4-7

Play #19: Rip 3 Inside Lead Left (Bomb)

Description: The inside lead play can be run weak as well as strong. When running weak, you can attack the playside bubble, which is the gap that is not covered by a down defender. Versus the overshifted 4-3, the bubble will often be in the B gap. Figure 4-8 illustrates the inside zone lead play to the openside.

Coaching Points:

- The offensive line must work to the playside jersey number of the down defender.
- With the bomb call, the center and playside guard can double-team the 1 technique.
- The back will read B gap to edge. He can bounce the football outside if the end slants inside.

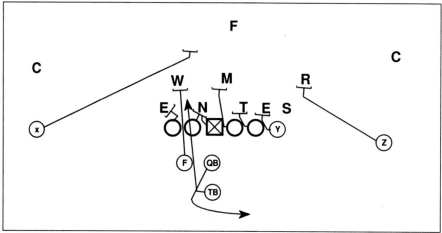

Figure 4-8

Play #20: Rip 2 Inside Lead Left (Bomb)

Description: To take away tendencies, you can align the fullback opposite the callside on zone lead. This keeps the defense from overplaying you to the side you align your fullback. In Figure 4-9, the fullback is aligned opposite the call, and leads onto the frontside inside backer.

Coaching Points:

- The offensive line must work to the playside jersey number of the down defender.
- The fullback must work quickly up to the playside backer.
- The back will read B gap to edge. He can bounce the football outside if the end slants inside.

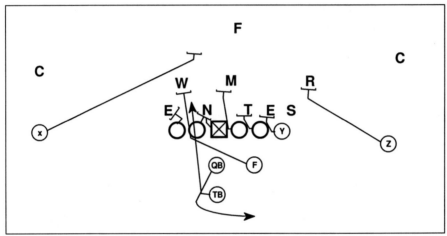

Figure 4-9

Play #21: Ron Bone Right Inside Lead Right Bus

Description: From the inverted bone formation, you can run zone either way. Your blocking rules do not change. Even though he is in the backfield, the tight end still blocks number 3 by rule. By tagging lead, the fullback knows he will block to the frontside. The bus call is a backside stay call to both the guard and the tackle. Bus tells the backside guard and tackle to stay. They will block solid. The bus call is used when you have enough blockers at the point of attack, or when you are worried about a backside threat. Figure 4-10 shows the fullback making a bomb call and blocking the playside linebacker.

Coaching Points:

- The offensive line must work to the playside jersey number of the down defender.
- The fullback will block the frontside inside or Mike backer.
- The back will read B gap to edge. He can bounce the football outside if the end slants inside.

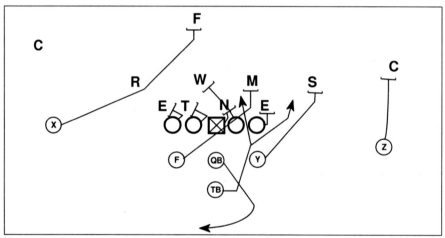

Figure 4-10

Play #22: Rip Bone X Over Inside Lead Left Halfback Seal (Bomb)

Description: Going into an unbalanced formation forces the defense to move extra bodies to the strongside. It also gives you an extra offensive lineman to the playside. From the bone, you can tag both lead and seal in the same play. The frontside back will lead on the frontside, and the backside back will seal the backside. In Figure 4-11, the inside lead play is shown from an unbalanced set. Both the bob and seal concepts are included in this play.

Coaching Points:

- The offensive line must work to the playside jersey number of the down defender.
- The fullback will block the frontside inside or Mike backer.
- The back will read B gap to edge. He can bounce the football outside if the end slants inside.

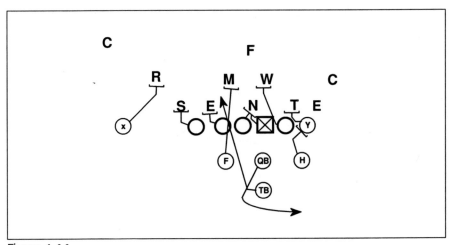

Figure 4-11

Play #23: Rip 7 Fake Fullback Jet Quarterback Inside Lead Right (Bomb)

Description: In addition to running a traditional inside lead play, you can run the lead off of virtually any running back action. A good complement to the jet sweep is to run the inside lead out the backdoor. Figure 4-12 illustrates the offense faking the ball to the fullback on jet sweep action, with the quarterback pulling the football and following the tailback through the backside B gap.

Coaching Points:

- The tailback must work downhill to the playside jersey number of the playside inside backer.
- The fullback will fake the jet sweep.
- The quarterback will have a long ride with the fullback before disengaging the mesh.

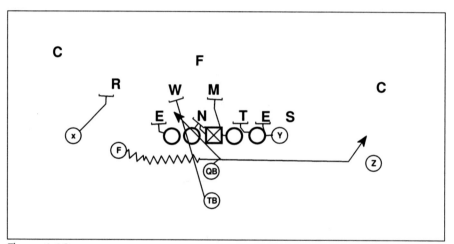

Figure 4-12

Play #24: Rip 7 Fake Fullback Jet Quarterback Inside Lead Right (Boss)

Description: When the quarterback runs the ball off the jet sweep, you can also make a boss call. Boss puts the tailback leading the quarterback up to the strong safety. This is effective when the backside defensive end is crashing hard on the jet play, giving you a soft edge. That means the tailback must block the force defender, giving your quarterback a crease to run the football.

Coaching Points:

- The tailback works to the edge, looking to pin or log the outside linebacker or strong safety.
- The fullback will fake the jet sweep.
- The quarterback will have a long ride with the fullback before disengaging the mesh.

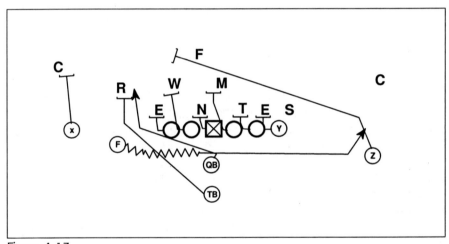

Figure 4-13

5

Power Concept

The power is a tremendous asset to have in any offense. In the pistol, you can run the power from a variety of formations. You can also use a variety of motion concepts. The power blocking scheme allows you to attack the defense in a multitude of ways. The power gives you a crease for your running back at the point of attack.

The power play can be run with a tight end, and to the openside. You can run the power with or without a lead back. The power gives you an opportunity to attack the C gap of the defense quickly in a downhill manner. Having a fullback who can kick out a defensive end or outside linebacker is a big key to the power being a successful play.

The rules for the offensive line are gap away. For example, if you call the power to the right, the offensive line will block the first gap to their inside. Additionally, when you coach your offensive line, you want to coach the uncovered/covered concept. This allows you to have two linemen working in tandem to drive the down defender to the linebacker. This zone combination concept is used by football teams at all levels. In addition, the backside guard will pull and wrap up into the first bubble to the playside. He is looking for first daylight to get vertical and block the backside linebacker.

In the two-back power, you will have your lead back, usually the fullback, lead on the end man on the line of scrimmage. The lead back must work tight to the heels of the offensive lineman so he can keep inside leverage of the end defender on the line. The fullback is aiming for the inside jersey number of that defender, and must avoid getting dug out at all costs. When running the power with no lead backer, or what is termed as one-back power, the tight end or tackle will base the end defender on the line of scrimmage. This allows you to account for each defender the defense has placed at the point of attack.

The backfield action on power is very basic, with both backs working to the playside. The fullback will immediately attack the inside jersey number of the defender he is assigned to block. The quarterback will take the ball through the third hand and step at 4 o'clock, working back to the tailback. The tailback will take an open step to the playside, then work downhill, attacking the outside foot of the playside tackle. He is reading playside bubble to the C gap. If the defense has a 1, 5, and 9 technique, the tailback will first read the B gap as he works downhill to the C gap. In Figure 5-1, the base two-back power play is shown versus an under front.

One of the dilemmas of running the power play is deciding which backer your frontside combination will track. A good rule to use is that you will never combo to a backer who is stacked, as they have too much leverage. A successful rule is to have the frontside combo to the A gap linebacker. If the frontside linebacker is wider than the A gap, the combo will work to the backside linebacker.

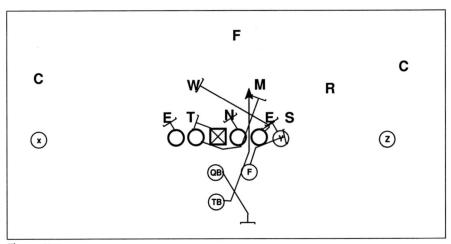

Figure 5-1

Play #25: Liz 3 Power Left

Description: This is the base two-back power play from a two-back pro formation. This is a downhill run play with great angles. The tight end and playside tackle will combo the end back to the Will linebacker. The center will block back on the defensive tackle.

Coaching Points:

- Your offensive line will get hip-to-hip on their combination blocks.
- The fullback must dig out the D gap; he cannot give up the inside.
- The playside receiver must block the alley runner.

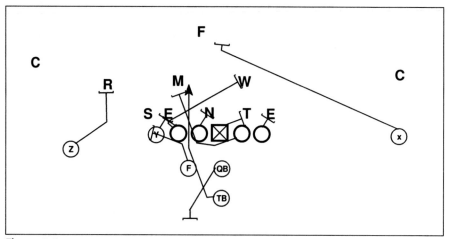

Figure 5-2

Play #26: Rip 2 Power Right

Description: Rip 2 puts the tight end to the right with the fullback stacked over the right tackle. On power, the fullback can cheat his alignment inside slightly to keep leverage on the D gap defender. Versus an overshift 4-3, the offense must make a decision on whether to double-team the 3 technique or the 7 technique. If the offense double-teams the 3 technique, they will not have as good of leverage on the Mike. Therefore, unless you are concerned with the 3 technique beating your guard, it is best to double-team the 7 technique. Figure 5-3 shows the tackle and tight end double-teaming the 7 technique, and the guard base-blocking the 3 technique.

Coaching Points:

- The center must be flat as he blocks back on the shade.
- The guard must get to the outside hip of the frontside 3 technique.
- The fullback must dig out the D gap player. He cannot give up the inside.

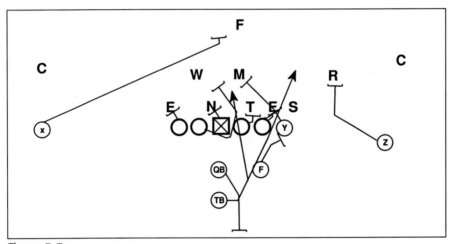

Figure 5-3

Play #27: Rip 3 Power Weak

Description: The power play can be run to the weakside as well as the strongside. Versus a 1 and 5 technique on the backside, you will be able to release your tackle to the inside linebacker. Your backside guard will wrap playside. Your fullback must get to the inside knee of the 5 technique. This is very effective when defensive ends run upfield.

Coaching Points:

- The fullback must get to the inside knee of the tackle.
- The center must stay flat when blocking back on the 3 technique.
- The wrapping guard must have his eyes open and block the first player in the opposite colored jersey.

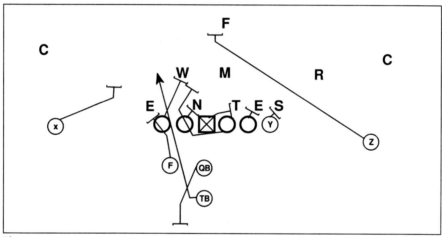

Figure 5-4

Play #28: Liz 2 Power Weak

Description: When you run the power weak versus an under front, your tackle can no longer release to the linebacker. The tackle and guard will now double-team the defensive tackle and climb to the linebacker. The center will block back on the noseguard. The backside guard will wrap and climb.

Coaching Points:

- The guard and tackle must get hip-to-hip.
- The backside tackle must protect his inside first.
- The running back will look to run off the inside hip of the block of the fullback.

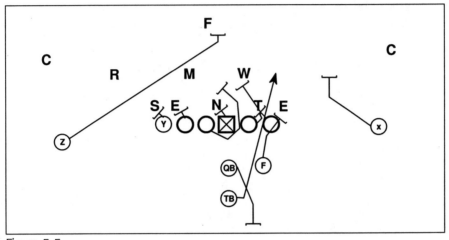

Figure 5-5

Play #29: Liz 8 Fap Power Weak

Description: Liz 8 puts the tight end to the left and the fullback aligned outside the Z-receiver. Fap motion puts the fullback across the formation. The quarterback will snap the ball when the fullback is over the guard. The fullback will shuffle as he gets to the backside guard. Aligning in a 3x1 look forces the defense to align to your strength. Using motion then forces the defense to adjust their front and/or coverage. Figure 5-6 shows the weakside power play with motion, and the defense adjusting to motion. The playside tackle will base a 4 or 4i defensive tackle. If the tackle slants hard, he will wash him down.

Coaching Points:

- The fullback will shuffle when he reaches the backside guard.
- The quarterback should snap the ball when the fullback is behind the frontside guard.
- The motion should be run at 70 percent of full speed.

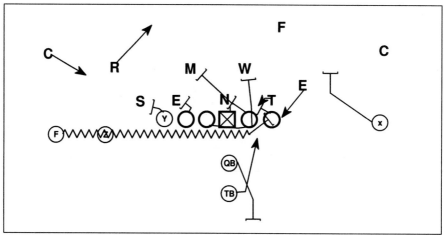

Figure 5-6

Play #30: Rip 6 Fip Power Right

Description: Aligning the fullback outside the box forces the defense to adjust. If the defense does not adjust, the quarterback would rise up and throw the ball to the fullback. If the defense does adjust, the fullback will motion back into the formation and kick out the end man on the line of scrimmage. Figure 5-7 shows the power with fullback motion into the formation versus a double Eagle front.

Coaching Points:

- The fullback will be in fast motion into the formation before shuffling with good leverage on his assignment.
- The offensive line will make a call to signify everyone is blocking back.
- The tailback read will remain unchanged.

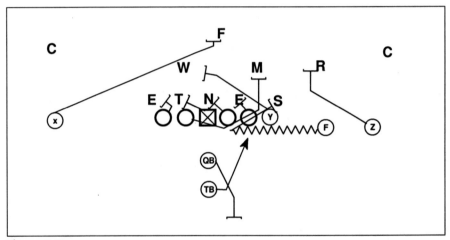

Figure 5-7

Play #31: Ray 2 Power Right

Description: Ray puts the tight end to the right, with the X and Z to the left. This is a traditional two-back twins closed look. Figure 5-8 shows power to the tight end side versus an under front with the defense rotated to the twins. The power play can be run both to the tight end and to the openside.

Coaching Points:

- The Y can widen his alignment to create a larger gap for running the ball.
- The fullback must dig out the D gap player, not giving up the inside.
- Versus an under front, the tailback is reading off the first frontside combo.

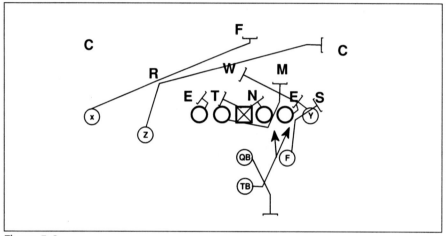

Figure 5-8

Play #32: Lee 3 Fap Power Weak

Description: Lee puts the tight end to the left side, and the X and Z opposite. Aligning the fullback to the tight end and motioning him weak allows you to run the power play to the twins rather than to the tight end. This is important as you want to force the defense to defend your run game both to the tight end and away. Figure 5-9 shows the power play to the weakside versus an overshift 4-3.

Coaching Points:

- The fullback can remain in motion; he does not have to reset.
- The quarterback must snap the ball when the fullback is inside the tackle.
- Your offensive line blocking rules remain unchanged.

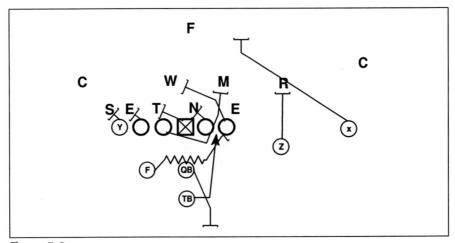

Figure 5-9

Play #33: Bone Y Power Right Gus

Description: The inverted wishbone is a great pistol formation. You can either put your tight end into the backfield, or you can bring in another running back. The frontside back will block the C gap player. If a "Y" tag is added, the Y is the lead blocker. With a "Gus" call, the backside guard will stay, and the extra back will wrap up to the linebacker. This allows the center and frontside guard to combo a head-up or strong shaded nose. Gus is a phonetic way of saying "Guard stay." Figure 5-10 shows the power play from the bone versus an even front defense with linebackers stacked.

Coaching Points:

- The Y must dig out the C gap defender.
- Your center and frontside guard must get movement on the nose.
- The mechanics of the play remain unchanged.

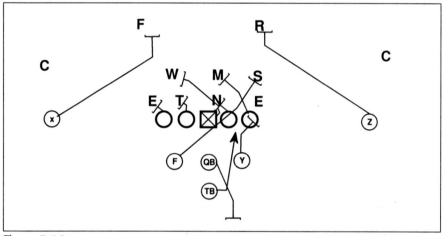

Figure 5-10

Play #34: Ron Bone Yap Power Left Gus

Description: You can use motion to bring the backside back to the playside. He will motion across the formation from the 2 to the 3 position, with the quarterback snapping the ball as the Y gets over the backside guard. This play is best run to the shade, as there is a natural bubble in the B gap. Figure 5-11 shows the power play from the inverted bone with motion.

Coaching Points:

- The fullback must be in front of the Y when the ball is snapped.
- Your center and frontside guard must get movement on the nose.
- The line blocks remain unchanged.

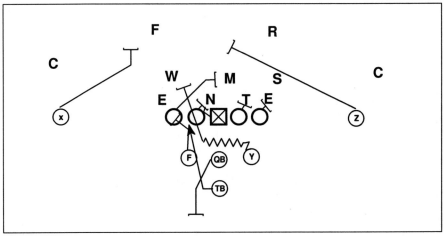

Figure 5-11

Play #35: Rip Bone 3 Yap Power Left Gus

Description: The bone can also be run with a tight end. Putting a tight end on the line of scrimmage forces the defense to have to matchup. This allows the offense to bring another running back into the game. In Figure 5-12, the power play is shown from the bone to the weakside.

Coaching Points:

- The fullback must be in front of the Y when the ball is snapped.
- Your center and frontside guard must get movement on the nose.
- The line blocks remain unchanged.

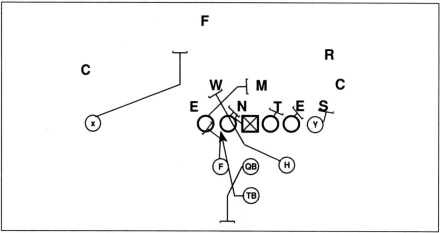

Figure 5-12

Play #36: Liz 6 Power Left vs. an Under Front

Description: Power can also be run from a one-back look. Instead of having a lead back kick out the playside end man on the line of scrimmage, the tight end will base-block the end man. Everything else remains unchanged. Essentially, you will zone the frontside and block back on the backside. The backside guard will pull and lead through the hole.

Coaching Points:

- The quarterback will open to the playside and roll the ball back to the tailback.
- The tight end will stay on the end man on the line.
- The receivers follow their blocking rules.

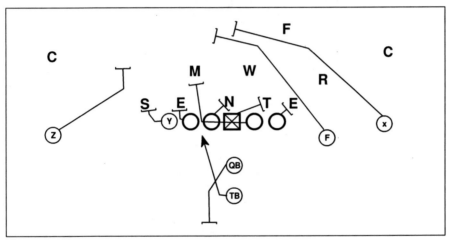

Figure 5-13

Play #37: Liz 3 Fake Zone Read Quarterback Power Left

Description: The quarterback power play can be run from both one- and two-back sets. The quarterback will ride the tailback through to the backside, as if it is zone read. The quarterback will use midline footwork, getting his eyes to the frontside B gap. The fullback will work inside and downhill to gain leverage on the end man on the line. He will then kick out the end man. Upon disengaging the mesh, the quarterback will run the power play.

Coaching Points:

- The quarterback must execute a long ride with the tailback.
- The fullback must get inside leverage on the end man on the line.
- The offensive line must get good movement.

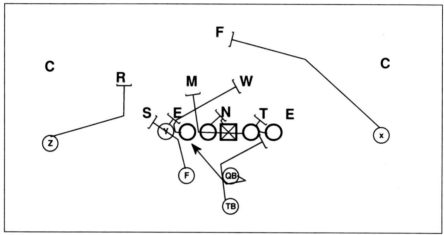

Figure 5-14

Play #38: Liz 6 Power Left vs. an Over Front

Description: The one-back power play can be run versus a variety of defensive fronts. Versus a college 4-3 defense, the tight end will base-block the 9 technique, and the playside tackle and playside guard will combo the 3 technique to the Mike backer. The pulling backside guard will block the Sam. Figure 5-15 illustrates the one-back power play from the pistol.

Coaching Points:

- The tailback has a two-way go.
- The pulling guard must be ready to attack the inside leg of the Sam linebacker.
- The backside tackle must step hard inside to keep the defensive end from crossing his face.

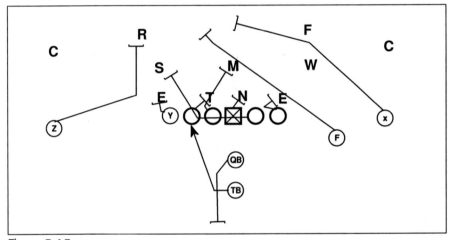

Figure 5-15

6

Sweep Concept

Every offense must be able to attack the defense from multiple flanks. Once you have success with your inside zone and power plays, the defense will begin to play much tighter. They will be more apt to play much thicker on the offensive linemen. They do this to restrict the inside gaps you are attacking.

To counter the defense defending against the inside run, the offense must attack the perimeter. One of the most important plays to attack the perimeter is the sweep play. The sweep is a very multiple concept that has been around for many years. The sweep play allows you to create an edge and attack the defense on the outside.

The sweep play is very simple for your offensive line. The frontside tight end will block down. He will work to the first defender to his inside. The playside tackle will block the first down lineman to the inside. If there is no down lineman in his inside gap, he will pull. The playside guard has the same rule. If he has a defender in his immediate inside gap, he will down block. If there is no defensive lineman to his inside, he will pull. The center, backside guard, and backside tackle will all rip-and-run, not letting any defender cross their face.

The footwork for the quarterback and tailback is designed to get the ball to the edge. The tailback will take a zone step to the playside and attack the inside leg of the tight end. As he approaches the heels of the offensive lineman, he will look to hit the edge, working one yard outside the block on the end man on the line of scrimmage.

Play #39: Rip 2 Sweep Right

Description: Versus an overshift 4-3, the tight end and tackle will both block down. The frontside guard will pull and look to lock the box. The playside receiver will work inside to block the force defender. If there is no force player in the alley, the receiver will work back to block the corner. The fullback will work off the edge and log the Sam. He must get to the outside shoulder and create an edge.

Coaching Points:

- The tight end and tackle must get great movement on their down blocks.
- The fullback must log the end man on the line.
- The tailback must press the heels of the tight end, and then bounce to the edge.

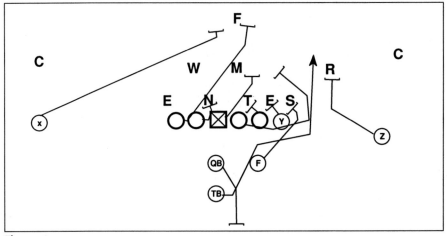

Figure 6-1

Play #40: Rip 2 Zip Crack Sweep Right

Description: The crack tag tells the wing or motion man to crack the end man on the line. The fullback will work up to the alley player. The pulling guard will block the first opposite-colored defender that crosses his face. This scheme tends to create a tremendous edge for the tailback to hit.

Coaching Points:

- The Z-receiver can align in the wing or go in motion toward the formation.
- The fullback must work to the alley.
- The puller must have his eyes up and his head on a swivel.

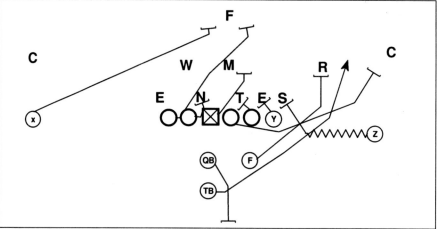

Figure 6-2

Play #41: Rip 2 Sweep Right vs. an Odd Front

Description: Versus an odd front, the frontside guard and tackle often will both be pulling. The frontside puller locks the box, while the backside puller works vertical to the corner. However, the backside puller must keep his head on a swivel. He will block the first opposite-colored jersey that crosses his face.

Coaching Points:

- Both the guard and tackle will pull by rule.
- The Z-receiver must get the force or alley player blocked.
- The tailback must press the heels of the offensive line before bouncing wide.

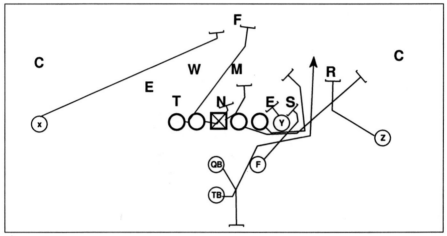

Figure 6-3

Play #42: Liz 4 Sweep Right

Description: When running the sweep play to the weakside, it helps to have a slot to that side who can down block on the defensive end. In Figure 6-4, this is illustrated with the fullback lined up in the slot and down blocking. The tackle then will pull and work to the first opposite color that crosses his face. Because there is no crack call, he will most likely be blocking the first force player. The second puller will block the corner.

Coaching Points:

- Both the guard and tackle will pull by rule.
- The X-receiver must work hard to block the safety running the alley.
- The tailback must press the heels of the offensive line before bouncing wide.

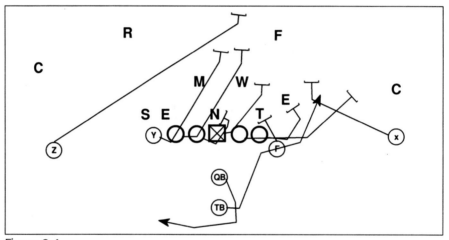

Figure 6-4

Play #43: Liz 3 Zip Crack Sweep Left

Description: Versus a 3-3 stack, the sweep play can be devastating. The Z-receiver motions into the formation and cracks the end man on the line of scrimmage. The tight end will block down on the defensive end. The tackle will pull and work to lock the box. The guard will pull and work to the corner. The fullback will be a third lead player, blocking the alley.

Coaching Points:

- The Z-receiver will crack the end man on the line.
- The defense will have three players in the alley to provide secondary run support.
- The tailback must press the heels of the offensive line before bouncing wide.

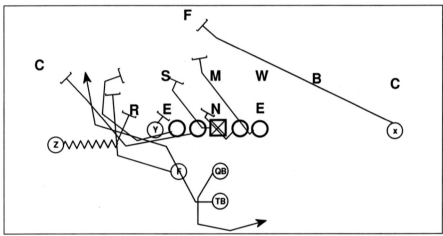

Figure 6-5

Play #44: Rex Crack Sweep Right

Description: The sweep play can be particularly effective from the bunch set. The Z and the tight end will block down. Versus an under front, the guard and tackle will both pull. The fullback will also be leading up into the secondary. This gives the offense three lead blockers in front of the ballcarrier.

Coaching Points:

- The Z-receiver will crack the end man on the line.
- The tight end will crack the defensive end.
- The guard and tackle will both pull by rule.

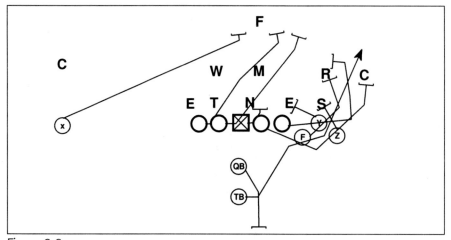

Figure 6-6

Play #45: Rip Bone Sweep Fap Sweep Right

Description: From the bone, the sweep is a very good play. The quarterback can have the option to run the play strong or weak based on numbers. The blocking rules do not change. In Figure 6-7, the tight end blocks down, and the tackle and guard pull. The center, backside guard, and backside tackle all rip-and-run. The fullback is in quick motion, and the quarterback calls for the snap as soon as the fullback clears him. You want the snap to be quick so the defense isn't able to adjust their front or rotate their secondary.

Coaching Points:

- The back must press the heels of the tight end before bouncing to the edge.
- The tight end will down block the defensive end.
- The guard and tackle will both pull by rule.

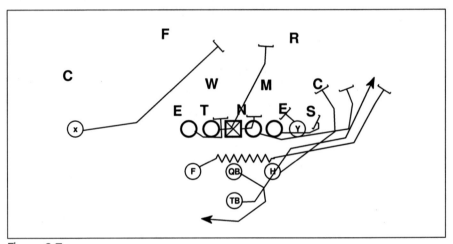

Figure 6-7

Play #46: Rip Bone Hap Sweep Left

Description: From the bone with a tight end, the play can also be run to the openside. Versus an under front, the tackle will block down, and the guard will pull. The guard will gain depth and log the defensive end. It is vital the quarterback get the ball to the tailback with some width.

Coaching Points:

- The X will stalk block the corner.
- The pulling guard will log the defensive end.
- The quarterback must get the ball to the tailback with width.

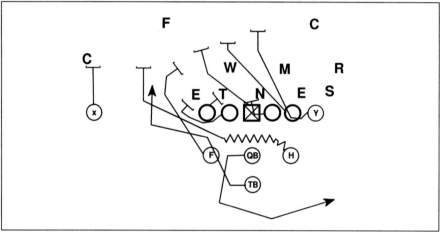

Figure 6-8

Play #47: Ray 3 Crack Sweep Left

Description: The sweep can be run from the twins closed look as well. Your inside receiver will tighten his split so he can crack or block down on the defensive end. With the #1 and #2 receivers to the playside working inside, the pulling guard will work out to the corner. The guard must get enough depth to work past the defensive end. The fullback will work through the alley to block the first opposite-colored jersey who may provide a threat.

Coaching Points:

- The X will crack the alley player.
- The Z will crack the defensive end.
- The backside of the line will rip, reach, and run.

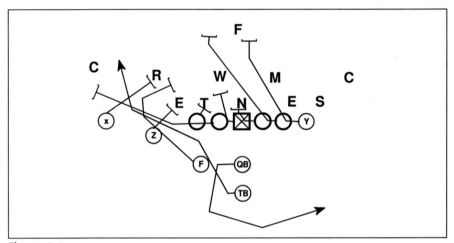

Figure 6-9

Play #48: Ray 2 Sweep Right

Description: The sweep play to the tight end side of your twins closed look can give you a tremendous edge to run the football. Versus a 50 front defense, the tight end will down block. Both the playside guard and tackle will pull. The playside tackle will gain depth, and then work to log the Sam. If the Sam runs upfield, the tackle will kick him out. The guard will pull and block the alley. The fullback will climb to the second level and lock the Mike in the box.

Coaching Points:

- The tight end must get movement on the defensive end.
- The playside tackle must work to log the Sam.
- The quarterback must get the ball to the tailback with width.

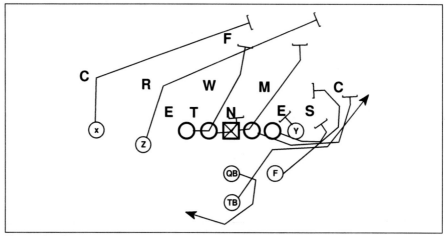

Figure 6-10

Play #49: Rip 7 Wing Sweep Right

Description: Aligning with a wing and slot can put the defense into a bind. The defense must be sure to put enough people to the side of the wing, while making sure as not to get outflanked to the slotside. Versus a 50 defense with a safety inverted to the weakside, the offense can flank the defense to the strongside. From this formation, your quarterback can flip the play strong or weak based on the defense. In Figure 6-11, the sweep play is illustrated to the wingside versus a 50 front.

Coaching Points:

- The Z must not let the Sam get upfield.
- The playside tackle must lock the box.
- The quarterback must get the ball to the tailback with width.

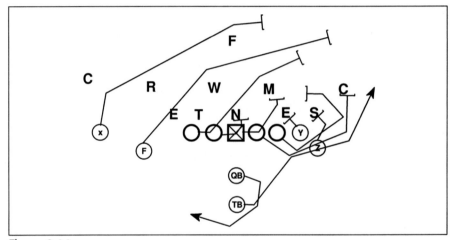

Figure 6-11

Play #50: Rip 5 Wing Crack Sweep Left

Description: If the defense does not rotate to the slotside, the offense can run the sweep in that direction. The slot will down block on the end, with the X-receiver cracking the playside inside linebacker. This allows the pulling tackle to climb to the safety. In Figure 6-12, the defense has a shade and 5 technique to the playside. This allows the guard to pull as well, and he can work to the corner.

Coaching Points:

- The X will lock the playside backer in the box.
- The pulling tackle can climb to the safety.
- The quarterback must get the ball to the tailback with width.

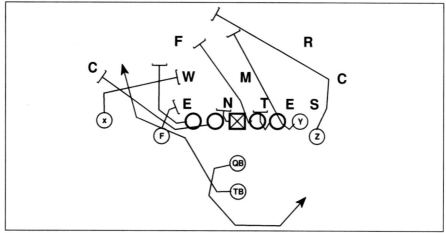

Figure 6-12

Play #51: Liz 3 Wing Cross Sweep Left

Description: The sweep play can also be run with cross-buck action. The quarterback will ride the fullback opposite the playside. The quarterback then pivots and gives the ball to the tailback.

Coaching Points:

- The tailback must pause slightly to allow the quarterback to fake to the fullback.
- The wing must beat the end man on the line for the defense.
- The pulling guard and tackle must have their eyes open.

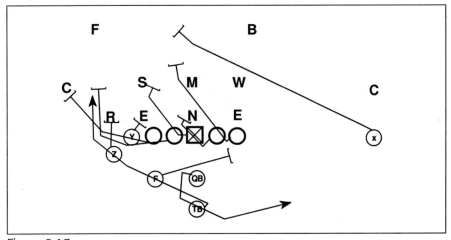

Figure 6-13

7

Isolation Concept

The isolation play is a concept designed to put the fullback isolated on one defender, usually an inside linebacker. The isolation play gives you an opportunity to run the football downhill in a physical manner. When the defense widens to take away your edge run game, your isolation plays allow you to attack the A or B gap quickly.

The offensive line blocking for the isolation play is relatively simple. They must know where the football is going, then position themselves with their hips into the hole. To be most effective, the offense wants to be able to double-team or zone combination block a defensive lineman.

The footwork for the quarterback and tailback is designed to get the ball to the back running downhill quickly. The quarterback will open at 45 degrees to the playside and roll the ball back. The running back will take a short zone step to the playside and get downhill. The quarterback will boot fake after giving the football.

Play #52: Rip 3 Iso Left

Description: Versus an overshift 4-3, the isolation play is best run to the weakside. This does not mean the isolation play can't be run strong, but the overshift 4-3 is designed to stop the tight end run. When running the isolation play, the offense wants to run the play to the A or B gap bubble. A great way to run the isolation play is to call the play with a check, and let the quarterback find the B gap bubble. The B gap bubble exists when the defense does not give you a B gap down defender. Figure 7-1 shows the isolation play run to the weakside in the B gap bubble.

Coaching Points:

- The center and left guard must get hip-to-hip on their combination block.
- The fullback must block the Will on the defensive side of the line of scrimmage.
- The tailback must get downhill quickly and cut off the block of the fullback.

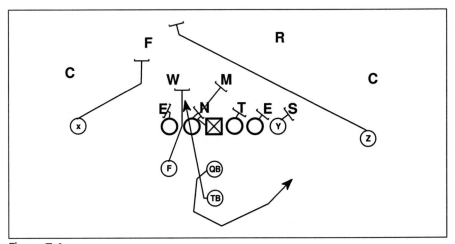

Figure 7-1

Play #53: Rip 6 Fip Iso Left

Description: Aligning in a trips look to the tight end side forces the defense to align to your strength. Then, you motion your fullback into the formation. The quarterback snaps the football when the fullback is behind the backside guard. The fullback then executes his isolation block on the playside inside linebacker. While the formation is different, this is essentially the exact same play as running the iso from the two-back gun with the fullback offset weak.

Coaching Points:

- The fullback must identify the playside inside linebacker quickly.
- The offensive line must get movement on the defensive line.
- The quarterback will boot fake out.

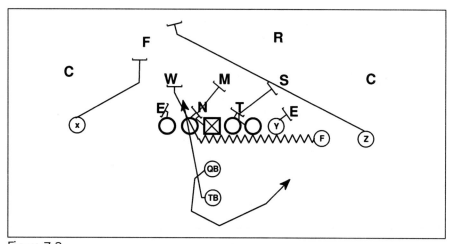

Figure 7-2

Play #54: Rip 6 Fip Iso Right

Description: Versus the college 4-3, the offense will have a rare C gap bubble to run the iso. With the exact same look as the previous play, the offense can run the iso strong. The fullback will align in as a twin to the trips side and go in motion into the formation. The quarterback will snap the ball as the fullback gets to the playside tackle. The fullback will then lead up on the playside inside linebacker. You can vary your motion to keep the defense off-balance.

Coaching Points:

- The fullback will isolate on the Sam linebacker.
- The offensive line wants to rotate their hips into the hole.
- The ballcarrier will cut off the block of the fullback.

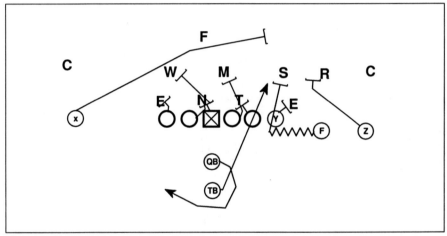

Figure 7-3

Play #55: Rip 2 Iso Right vs. 3-3 Stack

Description: Versus the 3-3 stack, the isolation play to the tight end creates conflicts for the defense. The fullback will isolate the Mike linebacker. The right tackle and tight end will double-team the defensive end to the Sam linebacker. The center and right guard will double-team the noseguard. The backside guard will block the backside linebacker.

Coaching Points:

- The fullback will isolate on the Sam linebacker.
- The offensive line wants to rotate their hips into the hole.
- The center and right guard must get movement on the noseguard.

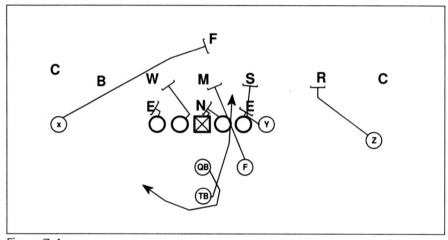

Figure 7-4

Play #56: Ron 2 Iso Right

Description: Flexing the tight end forces the defense to remove a player from the box. Often, this means the Sam linebacker will widen to leverage the #2 receiver. This leaves a six-man box, which is advantageous for the offense. Figure 7-5 illustrates the isolation play to the twins side with the fullback offset. The play is being run to the B gap bubble.

Coaching Points:

- The fullback will isolate on the Mike linebacker.
- The playside tackle must protect his inside first.
- The back will cut off the block of the fullback.

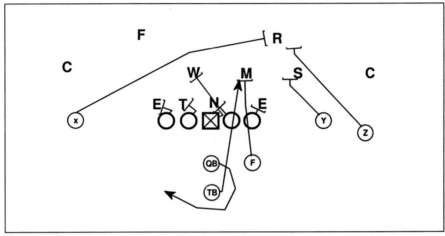

Figure 7-5

Play #57: Ron 2 Iso Right (A Gap Bubble)

Description: The isolation play can also be run to the A gap bubble. Typically, the A gap isolation is most effective when the defensive noseguard widens his alignment to a 2i or what is sometimes called a "G" alignment. This creates more space for the play in the A gap. Figure 7-6 illustrates the isolation play into the A gap bubble versus an even front defense.

Coaching Points:

- The fullback will isolate on the Mike linebacker.
- The playside guard and tackle must protect their inside gaps.
- The center and backside guard will combo the 1 technique to the backside backer.

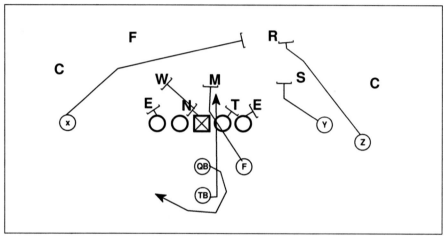

Figure 7-6

Play #58: Rex Iso Strong

Description: The bunch look forces the defense to defend the edge, which opens up opportunities to run the isolation play inside. When the defense widens to protect the edge, they leave a void inside. The isolation play allows the offense to attack the A or B gap void quickly. Figure 7-7 illustrates the isolation play to the bunch side.

Coaching Points:

- The fullback must work up to the linebacker to be isolated.
- The offensive line wants to rotate their hips into the hole.
- The center and right guard must get movement on the noseguard.

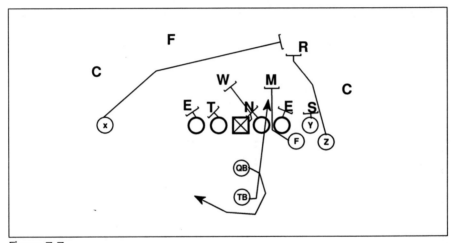

Figure 7-7

Play #59: Ray 2 Iso Strong

Description: When the offense aligns in a two-back twins closed look, the defense must decide where to declare their strength. If the defense rotates their secondary to the weakside, the isolation play is best run to the strongside. Figure 7-8 illustrates the isolation play to the strongside into the A gap bubble. The defense has rotated the secondary to the twins side. This allows the offense an advantage in the strongside A gap.

Coaching Points:

- The fullback will isolate the Mike linebacker.
- The center and left guard will combo the nose to the backside backer.
- The guard, tackle, and tight end must protect their inside.

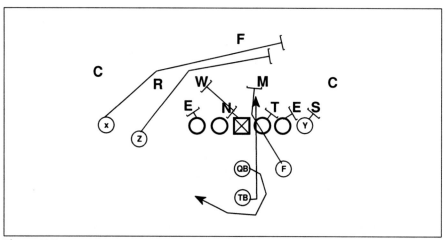

Figure 7-8

Play #60: Rip 2 Bison

Description: Bison is the backside isolation play. The backside isolation play has the fullback and tailback starting their path to one side, and bending the ball to the backside. In Figure 7-9, the fullback and tailback work to the right, then bend to the backside B gap. The backside isolation play works best when the defense gives you a 1 and 5 technique to the weakside.

Coaching Points:

- The fullback will work downhill three steps then bend backside.
- The left tackle must protect his inside gap.
- The tailback must be patient.

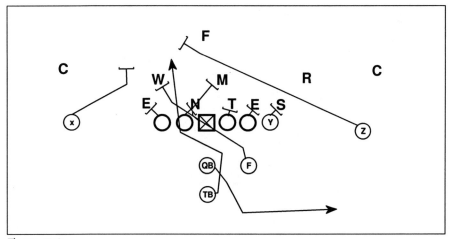

Figure 7-9

Play #61: Ron Bone Double Iso Left

Description: Several outstanding variations of the isolation play can be run from the three-back pistol look. As your opponent begins to widen their outside inverts or force defenders, you want to run the back toward the inside. Versus a 3-3 stack, the offense can outnumber the defense at the point of attack with the double isolation. The center and both guards will drive the nose into the Mike linebacker. The tackles will base-block the ends, protecting their inside gaps first. The fullback and halfback will both work up to the backers. This double isolation concept is very good against virtually any defensive front.

Coaching Points:

- The center and guards must get movement on the nose.
- The tackles must protect inside first.
- The tailback has a two-way go.

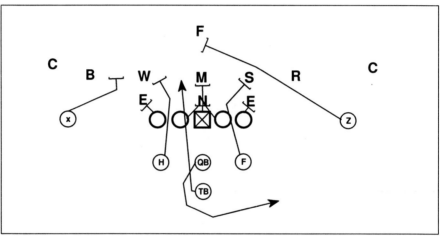

Figure 7-10

Play #62: Rip Bone Double Iso Left vs. Even Front

Description: The double isolation can also be run versus an even front. Ideally, the offense wants to run the isolation to the B gap bubble. Both offset backs will work up to isolate the two inside linebackers. With four down linemen and two backers in the box, the center and playside guard can stay on their double-team.

Coaching Points:

- The fullback and halfback will block the two inside backers.
- The center and left guard can stay on their double-team.
- The quarterback will check the play to the best numbers side.

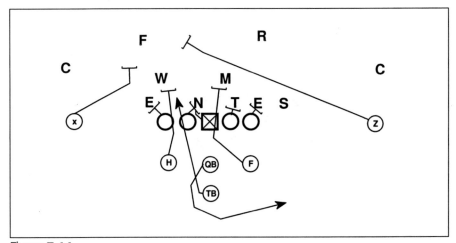

Figure 7-11

Play #63: Ron Bone Double Bison Nasty

Description: Bison can also be run from the three-back bone look. The nasty tag puts the frontside lead back on the end man on the line. If edge pressure is disrupting the play, the offense can tag nasty to put the frontside lead blocker on the edge.

Coaching Points:

- The halfback will block the edge pressure.
- The tailback must sell frontside first before the bend.
- The quarterback will boot fake out.

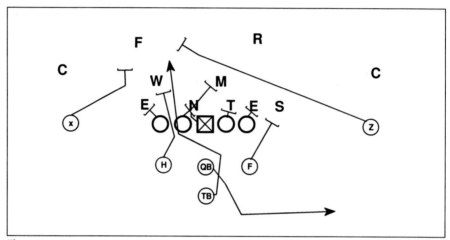

Figure 7-12

Play #64: Rip 6 Quarterback Iso Left

Description: The quarterback can be a runner in the pistol, which can give you a numerical advantage from your spread formations. Aligning in Rip 6 forces the defense to align to your tight end trips look. Upon taking the snap, the tailback attacks the Will linebacker. The quarterback takes the snap, takes one step back and shows the ball, and then runs up the heels of the lead blocker.

Coaching Points:

- The quarterback must pause to let the lead blocker clear.
- The tailback must be quick getting up into the hole.
- The center and left guard will combo up to the backer.

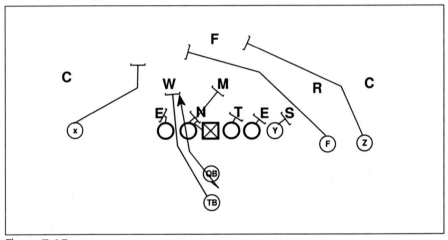

Figure 7-13

Play #65: Rip 5 Toz Quarterback Iso Left

Description: Sending the tailback in motion to the edge forces the defense to adjust. If the defense doesn't adjust, the quarterback will rise up and throw him the football. If the defense adjusts, the quarterback will take the snap and execute the isolation play weak. The fullback will wrap inside to block the playside linebacker.

Coaching Points:

- The quarterback must pause to let the lead blocker clear.
- The quarterback must read the rotation of the defense.
- The center and left guard will combo up to the backer.

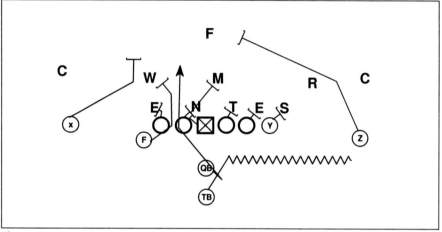

Figure 7-14

Play #66: Ron Bone Ride Sweep Quarterback Iso Left

Description: Part of the option game is running a wide sweep play with the backside back, with the quarterback reading a defender. A great complement to the wide sweep play is the quarterback isolation play out the backdoor. The quarterback rides the backside back on a wide sweep path. While this happens, the tailback sprints downhill to block the Will backer. The quarterback will then disengage the ride and run the isolation play through the B gap.

Coaching Points:

- The quarterback must get a long ride to force flow from the defense.
- The tailback must get downhill onto the playside backer.
- The frontside back will lead onto the edge to sell sweep action.

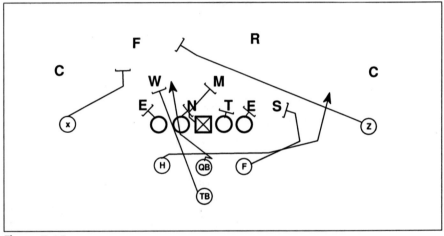

Figure 7-15

8

Trap Concept

The trap play is designed to take advantage of defenders who tend to run upfield. Several different trap concepts can be run from the pistol. The versatility of the pistol offense allows you to run different variations of trap concepts to keep the defense off-balance.

The first trap play to install is the quick trap of the first down defender past the offensive guard. If the first down defender past the guard is an outside shade of the guard, you will communicate a short call to the trapper. You can use any work you want, as long as it means something to your offensive linemen. If the player to be trapped is on or outside your tackle, you will need to make a long call. This tells the trapping lineman he will have a longer distance to travel before the trap block.

The rules for the offensive line are fairly simple. The player who is covered by the defender to be trapped will inside release to the linebacker. The trapper will open, rip, and run. He is looking to kick out the defender to be trapped. If the defender works to spill the trap block, the trapper will log the defender. This means he will log him inside.

Play #67: Liz 2 Tailback Trap Left

Description: The base trap play with the tailback is off of downhill action. The playside guard will alert short as the man being trapped is aligned in the B gap. The playside guard will climb to the Mike backer. The backside guard will open, rip, and run. The short alert lets him know the trap block will happen quickly. The backside tackle must protect the inside gap. He can pass set to influence, and then work out. The quarterback will push away from the midpoint and step to the mesh. He will ride the tailback and give the ball. Then, he will carry out a fake, sprinting to the edge. The fullback will sprint to the edge to hold the backside linebacker, and then climb to block the first opposite-colored jersey that shows. The tailback will run up the midpoint, engage in the mesh, and work straight downhill.

Coaching Points:

- The playside guard will make a short call.
- The backside tackle must keep inside leverage.
- The quarterback must be deceptive with his ball work.

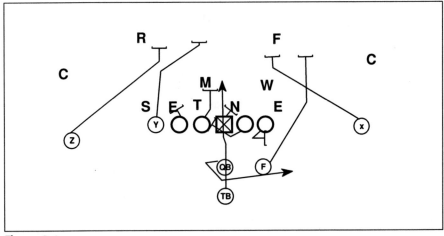

Figure 8-1

Play #68: Liz 2 Tailback Trap Left Fullback Seal

Description: If the backside linebacker is attacking over the top of the trap, you can release your backside tackle up to the backside inside backer. You can either read the defensive end, or you can have the fullback seal him. This is the same seal concept used on the inside zone. If the fullback is going to seal the defensive end, he must work to maintain inside leverage on the defensive end.

Coaching Points:

- The fullback must work to seal the C gap defender.
- The tackle must release, working inside of the backside backer.
- The tailback will work downhill.

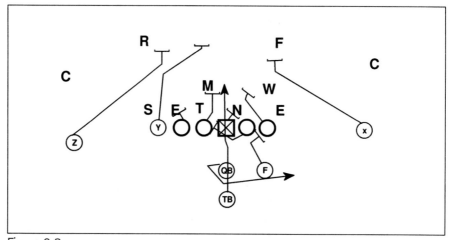

Figure 8-2

Play #69: Liz 3 Trap Left Wheel

Description: The trap play can also be run off of frontside action. Figure 8-3 shows the trap play off of one lead action from the backfield. The tailback will take a zone step, and then work downhill. The fullback will sprint to the edge and run a wheel route, working off the hip of the receiver. A coach in the box must watch the fullback to see if the defense covers him. If the defense is not covering him, the play-action will be set up.

Coaching Points:

- The tight end will release vertical and block the first support player.
- The center will block back on the nose.
- The tailback will run off the inside hip of the trapper.

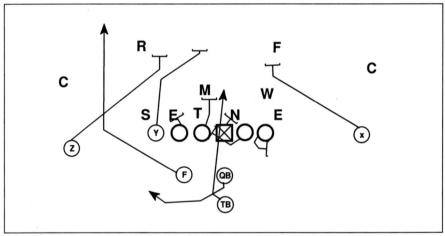

Figure 8-3

Play #70: Liz 6 Tailback Trap Left

Description: With zone read action, the offense can also run the trap. The quarterback will push away from the midpoint and mesh with the back. As he meshes, the back will cross in front of the quarterback. The offense can either block the backside defensive end, or the quarterback can read the defensive end. This gives the defense another concept to have to prepare for.

Coaching Points:

- The quarterback and tailback will mesh similar to the zone read.
- The ballcarrier must find the trapper and cut off his hip.
- The fullback, X, and Z will climb to the secondary and block support.

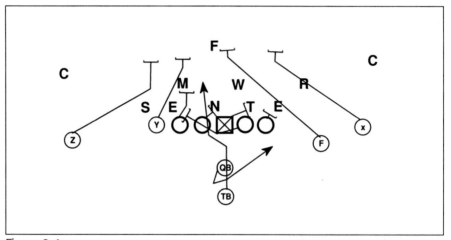

Figure 8-4

Play #71: Liz 2 Fullback Trap Weak

Description: The trap can also be run with the offset fullback. Figure 8-5 illustrates the fullback trap play. The quarterback will mesh with the fullback in front of him. He will ride the fullback across. The quarterback and tailback will then execute an option fake. This can also be run as a read play if the end is left unblocked. When there is a 1 and 5 technique to the playside, the tackle will make a long call to the trapper. This lets him know he will be trapping a C gap player.

Coaching Points:

- The center must block back on the 3 technique.
- The playside tackle will inside release to backer.
- The tailback will make a "ball" call while running in pitch relationship.

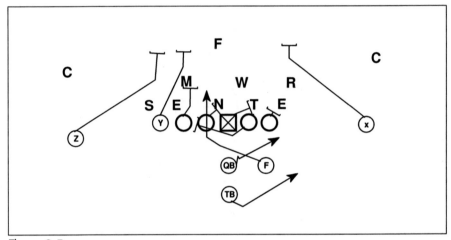

Figure 8-5

Play #72: Liz 2 Fullback Tackle Trap

Description: The trap play can also be run with the tackle being the trapper. When the tackle is the puller, the play becomes a read play. The quarterback will get his eyes on the defensive end lined up over the trapper. If the defensive end gets in the hip pocket of the trapper, the quarterback will pull the football. If the defensive end stays home, the quarterback will give the football.

Coaching Points:

- The frontside tackle will release to linebacker.
- The playside guard will block down on the 1 technique.
- This essentially becomes a triple option play.

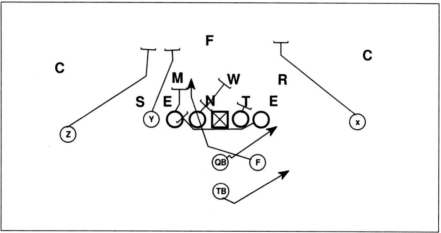

Figure 8-6

Play #73: Liz 2 Quarterback Trap Left

Description: The trap can also be run with the quarterback. Figure 8-7 shows the quarterback trap being run off wide sweep action. The quarterback will ride the fullback across, then pull the football and run the trap path. Nothing changes for the offensive line. This simple concept can take advantage of fast flow defenses.

Coaching Points:

- The fullback must sell the sweep.
- The center and backside guard combo to the backside linebacker.
- The tailback must be fast on his release to show full outside flow to the defense.

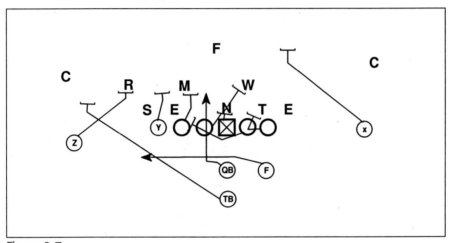

Figure 8-7

Play #74: Liz 5 Tailback Trap

Description: The tailback trap can also be run off of downhill zone action. The tailback will take a quick zone step, and then work at the outside hip of the guard. This takes his path slightly tighter than the inside zone play, but not noticeably so. He then bends his path behind the trapper. The flow creates a conflict for the defensive lineman, who tends to widen.

Coaching Points:

- The tailback must find the trapper.
- The center and left guard will combo the nose to the backside backer.
- The backside tackle must cut off the backside tackle.

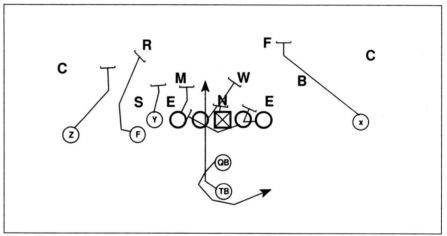

Figure 8-8

Play #75: Ron Bone Fap Tailback Trap

Description: The trap can also be run from the bone. This is a great complement to full flow zone from the three-back pistol. The motion by the fullback and lead path of the halfback creates flow for the defense. The flow can be to the playside or away. Figure 8-9 shows the trap being run to the backside of flow.

Coaching Points:

- The fullback and halfback must sell flow.
- The tailback must work downhill and find the trapper.
- The quarterback will sprint to the outside after giving the ball.

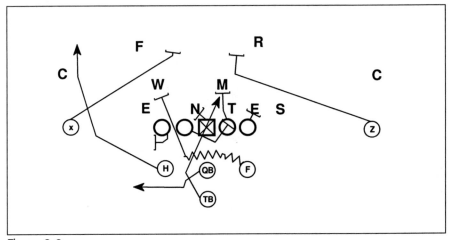

Figure 8-9

Play #76: Rip 7 Quarterback Trap Backside

Description: The quarterback trap can be run from a variety of formations and backfield motions. Figure 8-10 shows the quarterback trap being run off of a zone read fake to the tailback. The tailback must run a path at the outside hip of the backside defensive end. The quarterback in this case opens to the backside.

Coaching Points:

- The quarterback must sell the ride with the tailback.
- The playside guard must make a short or long call.
- The quarterback must have good ball security.

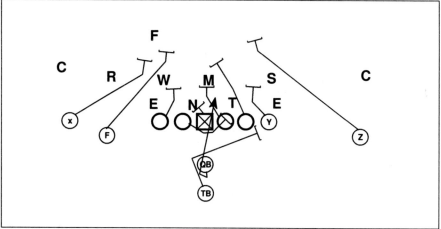

Figure 8-10

Play #77: Rip 7 Quarterback Trap Frontside

Description: The quarterback can open to the backside. When the quarterback opens frontside, he will ride the tailback backside. This gives a cross key to the Mike linebacker, giving the guard a chance to get him walled.

Coaching Points:

- The quarterback will open to the frontside.
- The frontside guard will make a long or short call.
- The tailback will block the backside end.

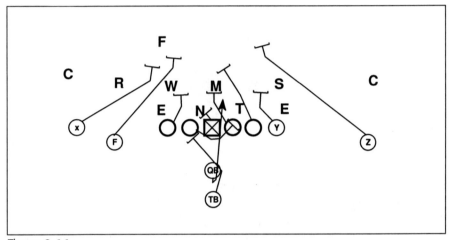

Figure 8-11

9

Counter Concept

The counter play is designed to take advantage of fast flow defenses. The counter play is a staple of the pistol offense. When defenses start to flow fast to stop your full or fast flow run game, they leave themselves exposed for the counter play.

On the counter play, the offense will pull the backside guard and tackle. The guard will pull and kick out the designated defender, and the tackle will pull and lead through to the second level. The frontside of the counter play will simply zone toward the backside. They must work to create flow for the defense. This helps to set up the counter play.

The tailback will take a zone step, then two downhill steps. The quarterback will open at 45 degrees and show the ball in front of him. As he gets to the tailback, he will give the ball off his back hip. As he gives the football, he must dip his hip. This helps to set up the counter boot play.

Play #78: Rip 3 Counter Trey Right

Description: The counter play is an outstanding complement to the full flow run game weak. If the defense is playing fast to full flow weak, the offense can come back with a counter play. Figure 9-1 shows a base counter play from a two-back pro pistol look. The guard will kick out the end man on the line of scrimmage. The tackle will pull and lead through.

Coaching Points:

- The quarterback and tailback must sell zone weak.
- The fullback must block the defensive end, just like his seal technique.
- The tailback must get in the hip pocket of the tackle.

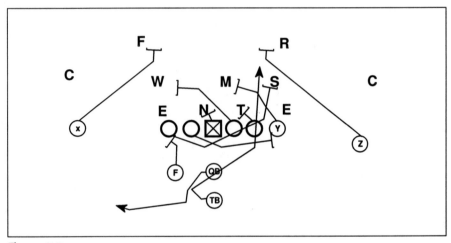

Figure 9-1

Play #79: Rip 3 Counter Trey Right vs. Under

Description: Versus an under front, the offense has a decision to make. The guard can either kick out the 5 technique or the 9 technique. If the 5 technique is coming upfield quickly, then it is best to kick out the 5 technique. If the 5 technique tends to squeeze, the offense would down block the 5 and kick out the 9 technique. The counter trey is illustrated in Figure 9-2 with the defensive end being kicked out.

Coaching Points:

- The guard must be flat on his pull.
- The backside tackle who is pulling must see daylight.
- The fullback must dig out the backside C gap.

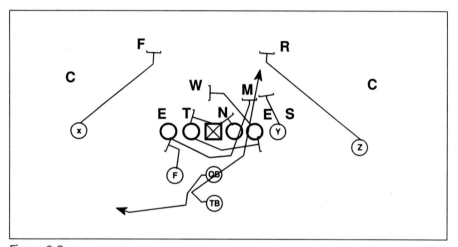

Figure 9-2

Play #80: Rip 2 Counter Left (Weak)

Description: The counter is also a good play to run to the weakside. The mechanics of the play stay the same as with the counter strong. The one difference is the speed at which the play hits. The counter play weak tends to hit much tighter than the counter play strong. Figure 9-3 shows the counter play to the weakside. The counter weak is a great complement to strongside full flow run game.

Coaching Points:

- The fullback and Y must secure the backside.
- The frontside tackle must get a good down block.
- If the defensive end to the playside squeezes, the pulling guard must log the defensive end.

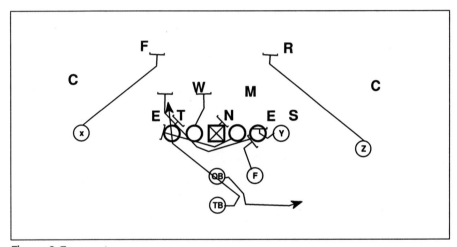

Figure 9-3

Play #81: Lou 6 Counter Right Read

Description: The counter can also be run as a counter read play. The quarterback will read the backside defensive end who is unblocked. This allows you to account for the backside defensive end when running the counter from a one-back set. The quarterback will use midline footwork and reach the ball deep. His eyes will go to the backside defensive end. If the defensive end squeezes and chases, the quarterback will pull the football and replace him. If the 5 technique does anything else, the quarterback will give the football. Figure 9-4 illustrates the counter read.

Coaching Points:

- The quarterback must get his eyes on his read.
- The tailback will come off the midpoint and work across the bow of the quarterback.
- The blocking does not change.

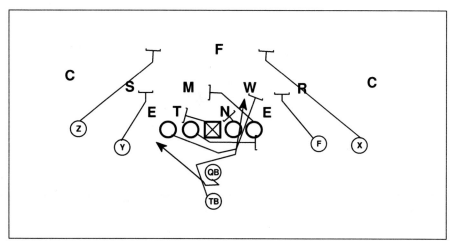

Figure 9-4

Play #82: Lou 3 Counter Right Read Option

Description: The counter read can also be run as a triple option play. The quarterback will read the backside defensive end for his give keep read. The fullback will be the back with whom the quarterback will mesh, and the tailback will become the pitch man.

Coaching Points:

- The Y must get a good block on the edge.
- The tailback must make a "ball" call while running with the quarterback.
- The quarterback must practice good ball security.

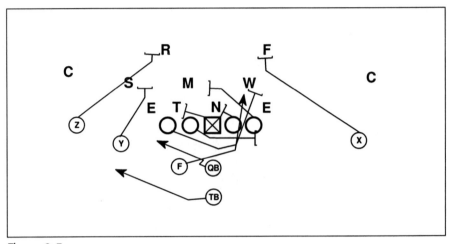

Figure 9-5

Play #83: Lou 2 Quarterback Counter Right

Description: The counter play can also be run as a designed keep for your quarterback. This is a great play to run with your regular personnel or a wildcat set. Once you establish the running game with your fullback and the defense flows quickly, your quarterback can ride the back and pull the football, running the counter. The tailback sprints to the playside and makes a "ball" call. This helps to hold the alley player. Figure 9-6 illustrates the quarterback counter play from a two-back set.

Coaching Points:

- The quarterback must have a good ride with the fullback.
- The tailback must make a "ball" call.
- The receivers must do a great job of blocking the force players.

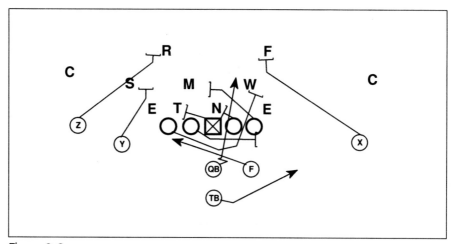

Figure 9-6

Play #84: Liz 6 Quarterback Counter

Description: The quarterback counter can also be run from a one-back set. The quarterback will step off the midpoint and mesh with the tailback. The tailback will work to gain width to hold the backside defensive end. The quarterback will work downhill off the block of the tackle.

Coaching Points:

- The quarterback must step off the midpoint to mesh.
- The offense can kick out the 7 technique or the 9 technique.
- The tailback must sprint to the edge as if he is running sweep.

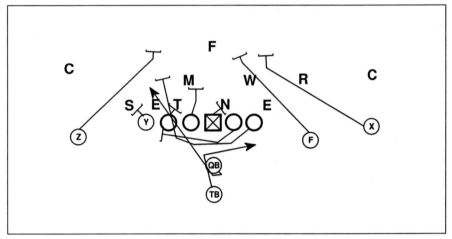

Figure 9-7

Play #85: Liz 7 Quarterback Counter Read Cheetah

Description: Cheetah is an alert that you are reading a backside player on a quarterback run. Figure 9-8 shows the cheetah play off counter action. The quarterback is reading the backside end. If he gets in the hip pocket of the pullers, the quarterback will give the ball to the tailback, who is sprinting wide. This play should be run from a 3x1 set with a defense rotated strong. This takes away the alley player to the cheetah side. The read player is circled in Figure 9-8.

Coaching Points:

- The quarterback must step off the midpoint to mesh.
- The quarterback must get his eyes to his read.
- The tailback must be fast to the edge.

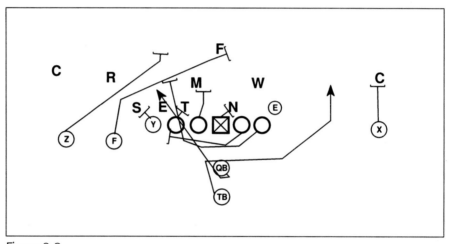

Figure 9-8

10

Belly Concept

The belly series gives you an opportunity to get the football into the hands of your fullback and tailback with great angles. The belly play can be installed with base blocking, or with the guard kicking out the end man on the line of scrimmage. The belly series can be run strong or weak.

The belly series consists of the dive phase, keep phase, pitch phase, and pass phase. When the defense has their end coming upfield, the belly becomes a very good play. The playside tight end and tackle will block down, with the playside guard pulling and kicking out the defensive end. This creates a seam for the back to run.

When the defensive end begins to spill, or come underneath your kickout block, the keep phase comes into play. The kickout block now becomes a log block. This means the guard will pin the defensive end inside. The running back will now work outside the puller and block the next opposite-colored jersey. The quarterback will then keep the football.

If the alley player is getting to the quarterback and tackling him on the keep phase, the pitch phase comes into play. This requires two backs, and the second back becomes the pitchman. If the alley player attacks the quarterback, the quarterback will pitch to the second back. This forces the defense to play assignment football. The belly is a tremendous series in short- and medium-yardage situations.

Play #86: Rip 7 Wing Belly Right

Description: The belly play is solid to the overshift 4-3. The tackle and tight end have great leverage to down block the playside defensive end. The center and backside guard combo the backside nose to the Will. The wing is responsible for locking the Mike in the box. The quarterback reverse pivots and rides the back for two counts before giving the ball. The quarterback then sprints to the edge. The tailback will take a jab step playside, then attack the inside leg of the tight end. He makes a deep, soft pocket to receive the handoff. He then finds his puller and runs off his backside.

Coaching Points:

- The center and left guard must get hip-to-hip on their combination block.
- The guard must work to the inside number of the Sam.
- The tailback must run with his eyes open.

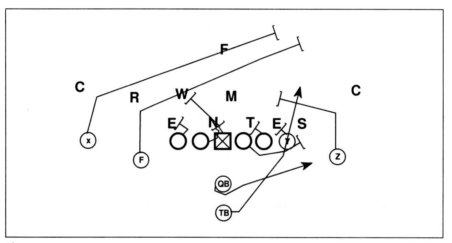

Figure 10-1

Play #87: Rip 7 Wing Belly Guard Right vs. 4-3 Wide

Description: The belly is a great play to run versus the college 4-3. The offense has great angles to the playside. The tight end releases to the Mike linebacker and walls him inside. The wing is responsible for getting the outside half of the Sam blocked. The pulling guard will kick out the end man on the line.

Coaching Points:

- Versus a college 4-3, the back must tighten his path to help the Z wall the Sam.
- The tackle must do a great job of creating space on his down block.
- The quarterback must sprint outside after giving the football.

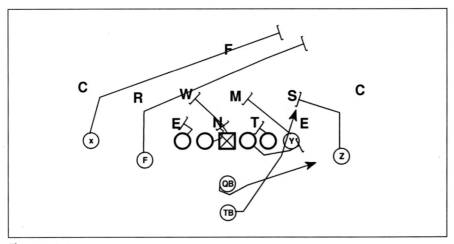

Figure 10-2

Play #88: Rip 7 Wing Belly Right vs. Under Front

Description: Versus the under front, the tight end will block down on the 5 or 7 technique. The playside tackle must make sure the center secures the playside noseguard before working to the backside backer. The wing has a great angle on the Mike. The key to the play is the tight end getting movement on the defensive end to create space.

Coaching Points:

- The guard must look to drive the Sam outside.
- The wing must wall the Mike.
- The ballcarrier will cut off the block of the guard.

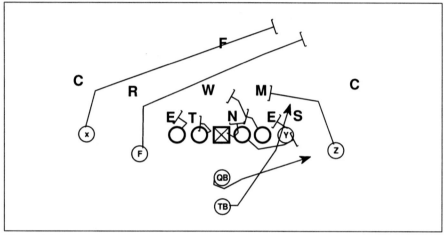

Figure 10-3

Play #89: Rip 2 Belly Iso Right

Description: The belly isolation play gives you another blocker at the point of attack. When the defensive end to the strongside is getting upfield, the belly isolation play gives you leverage in the C gap.

Coaching Points:

- The fullback will isolate on the Sam linebacker.
- The playside guard must work through the inside jersey number of the defensive end.
- The tailback will cut off the block of the fullback.

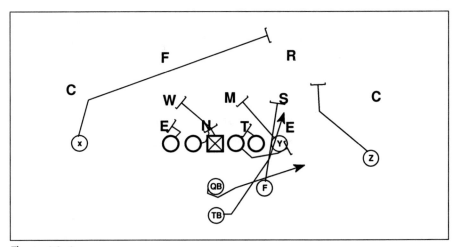

Figure 10-4

Play #90: Rip 3 Belly Iso Left

Description: The belly isolation play can also be run to the weakside. The tackle will block down on the 3 technique, and the guard will pull and kick out the end. This is a great way to attack a wide defensive end away from the tight end. The fullback will isolate the playside linebacker, looking to lock him in the box.

Coaching Points:

- The fullback will lock the Will linebacker inside.
- The playside tackle must get movement on the 3 technique.
- The quarterback will sprint to the edge after giving the football.

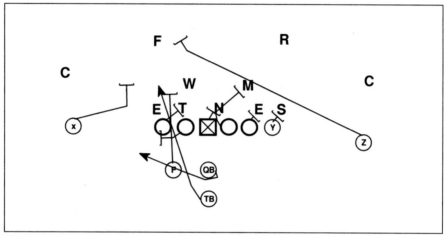

Figure 10-5

Play #91: Rip 5 Belly Zone Left

Description: The belly play can also be run with zone blocking. The offensive line will use their zone blocking rules. The back will look for the first daylight, attacking the outside edge of the playside bubble. This is a great play to run to the openside versus a nose and 5 technique. The center is key, as he must block the nose.

Coaching Points:

- The center must get to the playside thigh of the nose.
- The playside guard and tackle must secure any stunts from the end and Will.
- The fullback will block the alley player.

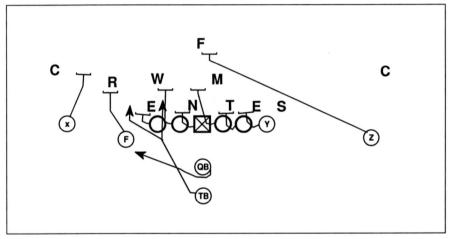

Figure 10-6

Play #92: Ricky 5 Belly Zone Right

Description: The belly can also be run to the strongside with zone blocking. This is a great look from a trips closed look when the defense gives you an under front.

Coaching Points:

- The tailback will attack the outside edge of the bubble.
- The quarterback will sprint off the edge after giving the football.
- The quarterback can check the play either way based on alignment.

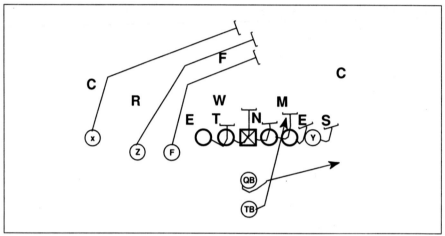

Figure 10-7

11

Reverses and Special Plays

Every offense needs to have special plays to incorporate into their game plan. Every concept should have a play-action component, and select concepts also need a reverse. Running a reverse can change the momentum of a football game. A successful trick or special play can result in a game-changing moment.

Special plays need to fit into your regular offensive system. A reverse is much more effective if it is run off a concept that is already a part of your offensive package. Each team should have two to three special plays in their game plan for that particular week. Your goal should be to run your reverse as early in a game as possible. Once you run a reverse or special play, you slow your opponent's pursuit down.

Play #93: Rip 2 Zip Z Reverse Seal Left

Description: The inside zone play provides an opportunity to run the Z reverse. The Z-receiver goes into motion into the formation. The quarterback snaps the ball when the Z-receiver is one yard outside the tight end. The offensive line follows their inside zone blocking rules. The word "seal" tells the fullback he will take his seal path backside. Because the play is a reverse, he will log the backside C gap player. The quarterback will fake to the tailback, then turn his back to the defense and give to the Z-receiver. After giving the ball, he sprints outside to where the Z came from. You can also fake the Z reverse with this series.

Coaching Points:

- The offensive line must execute their normal inside zone blocking.
- The quarterback and tailback must sell inside zone.
- The fullback will log the backside defensive end, sealing him inside.

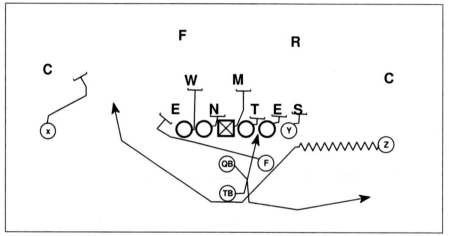

Figure 11-1

Play #94: Rip 2 Zip Z Reverse Guppie Seal Left

Description: Guppie is a variation where the guard pulls playside. Since the reverse is left, the left guard will pull and block the corner. This allows the receiver on the reverse side to wall the near backer. The Guppie guard will take one zone step before pivoting and working to the corner.

Coaching Points:

- The guard pulling must take one zone step to sell the play.
- The offensive line must be fast to encourage flow.
- The quarterback must turn his back to the defense.

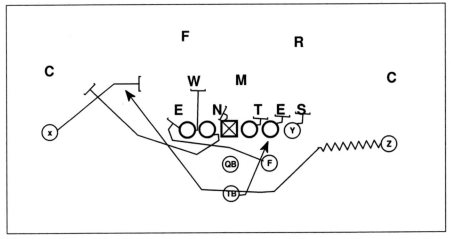

Figure 11-2

Play #95: Rip 5 Fullback Reverse Right Tackle Circle

Description: The reverse can also be run off the belly G series weak. Tagging "tackle circle" tells the tackle to the reverse to circle back around and seal the end man on the line of scrimmage. The quarterback again will fake the tailback, and then turn his back to the defense when he gives to the fullback.

Coaching Points:

- The fullback will take one step upfield before working to the quarterback.
- The tackle must get the Sam sealed.
- The tailback must make it look like he has the football.

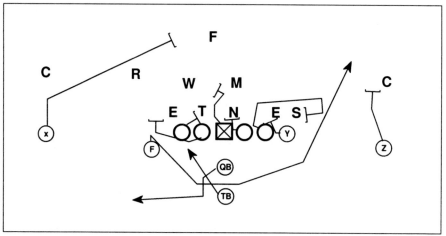

Figure 11-3

Play #96: Rip 5 Wing Fullback Jet Z Reverse

Description: The jet sweep is a great play to force the defense to defend the entire field. To stop the jet, the defense needs to rotate quickly to the speed of the jet back. Off the jet, the reverse to the wing becomes a very good football play. The fullback will take the handoff from the quarterback. He will then give the ball to the Z on an inside handoff. You can have the backside guard pull to lock the box for the reverse, or you can block the reverse base.

Coaching Points:

- The Z will take an inside handoff.
- The quarterback can lead block after giving the football.
- The tailback sprints to the edge like he is leading the jet.

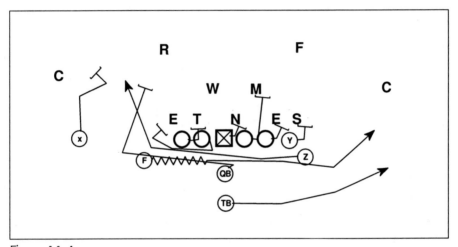

Figure 11-4

Play #97: Rip 3 Inside Flea Flicker

Description: When the defense begins to aggressively attack the zone, you can run the flea flicker. This takes advantage of the secondary coming up quickly in run support. The quarterback will hand the ball to the tailback, who will take three steps and then pitch the ball back to the quarterback. The quarterback then throws the football down the field.

Coaching Points:

- The fullback runs a wheel route.
- The offensive line blocks inside zone.
- The quarterback must be ready to throw the football upon receiving the pitch.

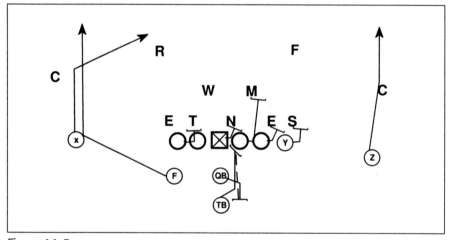

Figure 11-5

Play #98: Rip 3 Zap Z Counter Reverse

Description: The counter reverse is another way to take advantage of fast flow defenses. The quarterback will fake the zone lead play to the tailback, and then he will turn his back to the defense and give the football to the Z. With the counter reverse, the center and tackle will pull to lead the Z. Figure 11-6 illustrates the counter reverse.

Coaching Points:

- The Y must get a good down block on the send.
- The tackle must lock the Sam.
- The quarterback must turn his back to the defense.

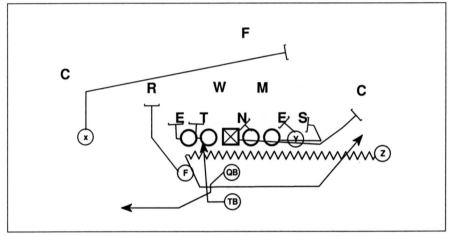

Figure 11-6

Play #99: Liz 1 Stack Fullback Wham Left

Description: The wham play is a great variation of the trap. The wham concept has the fullback trap blocking the 1 technique. If the 1 technique squeezes, the fullback will log him. The tailback must read the block of the fullback. This is a great concept if you are using heavy sets.

Coaching Points:

- The fullback must read the movement of the nose for his log or kick out.
- The tailback must read the block of the fullback.
- The quarterback will sprint out after giving the football.

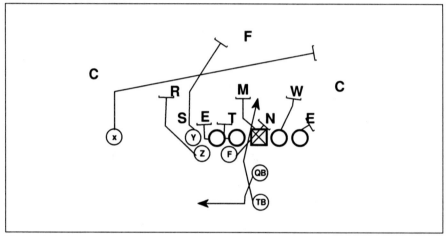

Figure 11-7

Play #100: Rip Bone Z Crack Reverse

Description: The reverse can also be run from the bone. The quarterback will fake the zone to the tailback, before turning his back to the defense and giving the ball to the Z-receiver. The quarterback will then sprint to the edge. The crack call puts the X-receiver on the ally player, with the fullback working to the corner.

Coaching Points:

- The X will crack the alley player.
- The quarterback must turn his back to the defense to give the ball to the Z.
- The tailback must carry out a good fake.

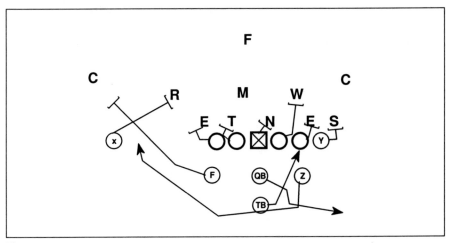

Figure 11-8

Play #101: Rip Bone Fake Z Quarterback Trap

Description: Off the Z reverse, the offense can run quarterback trap. From Rip bone, the quarterback will fake the ball to the tailback, who will lead up on the playside backer. The quarterback will then turn his back to the Z and fake the reverse. After a one-count pause, he will turn back to the line of scrimmage and run the A gap trap. The key is the ability of the quarterback, Z, and tailback to carry out good fakes. Deception makes this series work. Figure 11-9 illustrates this concept.

Coaching Points:

- The tailback will block the playside linebacker.
- The quarterback must use great deception.
- The backside of the offensive line will reach to sell the reverse.

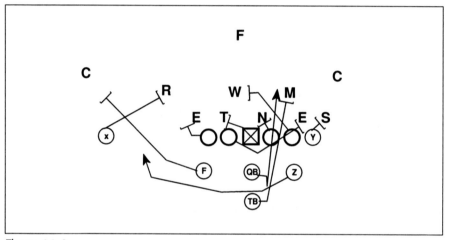

Figure 11-9

About the Author

James Vint has been both an offensive and defensive coordinator at the high school and collegiate levels, and currently is defensive line coach and special teams coordinator at Coronado High School, a 5A school in Lubbock, Texas. Previously, Vint was an assistant coach at Truman State University and the offensive coordinator at Iowa Wesleyan College, where he and his offensive staff were on the forefront of developing the pistol offense.

Prior to his stint at Iowa Wesleyan, Vint served on the coaching staff at Christopher Columbus High School in the Bronx, New York, where he helped turn around a gridiron program that had a 20-game losing streak. In his second season at Columbus, the Blue Steel qualified for the playoffs for the first time in school history, a feat that they achieved four times over a six-year period. During his five seasons on the Columbus staff (2000-2004), the Blue Steel offense averaged 256 yards per game on the ground.

Vint is a widely sought-after speaker at clinics throughout the country, and has been featured on a number of well-received instructional DVDs on the pistol offense.